101 MakeOver Minutes

Tammy Bennett

HARVEST HOUSE PUBLISHERS

EUGENE, OREGON

Cover by Garborg Design Works, Savage, Minnesota

Cover photo © Fancy Photography / Veer; back-cover author photo © Briar Photography

---

Advisory

Readers are advised to consult with their physician or other medical practitioner before implementing any suggestion that follows.

This book is not intended to take the place of sound medical advice or to treat specific maladies. Neither the author nor the publisher assumes any liability for possible adverse consequences as a result of the information contained herein.

---

101 MAKEOVER MINUTES
Copyright © 2007 by Tammy Bennett
Published by Harvest House Publishers
Eugene, Oregon 97402
www.harvesthousepublishers.com

Library of Congress Cataloging-in-Publication Data
Bennett, Tammy.
  101 makeover minutes / Tammy Bennett.
    p. cm.
  ISBN-13: 978-0-7369-1992-0 (pbk.)
  ISBN-10: 0-7369-1992-9 (pbk.)
  1. Christian women—Religious life. 2. Women—Health and hygiene. I. Title. II. Title: One hundred and one makeover minutes. III. Title: One hundred one makeover minutes.
  BV4527.B44 2007
  248.8'43—dc22   2007002514

Printed in the United States of America

07 08 09 10 11 12 13 14 15 /VP-KB / 10 9 8 7 6 5 4 3 2 1

To my husband, who makes my life beautiful and complete—
Happy Silver Anniversary

xxoo…
Tammy

Contents

Make Me Over

Women of all shapes, sizes, colors, and ages love to look and feel their absolute best. It's a proven fact that when you look better, you feel better. And when you feel better, you act more confidently. But how do you get the confidence to start the "looking better" process?

Many women want makeovers, but very few have the nerve to try them. And those who do often lack the motivation to keep up the changes. Statistics show that the vast majority of those who receive total head-to-toe makeovers rarely keep them up. The *Oprah Winfrey Show* has featured many makeovers through the years, and the follow-up segments are staggering. Very few have kept up the makeover process. Most women fell back into the same old rut they were in before.

Why do makeovers so seldom "take"? I believe it's because a successful makeover begins on the *inside*. If we change the outside without changing the inside we still see ourselves the same as we did before the makeover took place. Sure, the outer changes will last for a temporary period of time—and during that phase you may look and feel great—but if you don't make over the *inside,* the good feeling will eventually dissipate. You'll end up going back to your old way of living, which will take you back to the same old regimen you followed prior to the makeover.

Here's the key: The makeover secret is found in *looking good from the inside out.* This concept might seem a bit overwhelming, but with the Word of God and the hints in this book, help is on the way. You're about to learn how to apply the truth of the Scriptures along with tried-and-true beauty secrets to help you receive a lasting makeover—one that won't fade away but will instead intensify over the course of time. Yes, in this case time *is* on your side—time to grow, mature, and develop an everlasting beauty routine in a series of MakeOver Minutes.

101 MakeOver Minutes is designed to be both easy to use *and* to bring about life-changing results. It's divided into short, simple segments that will transform both your body and your soul. Each chapter is designed around a single point of interest that will inspire, enlighten, and challenge you from the inside out. You also have a space to write a prayer note to God, record praises, or give thanks and count your blessings—even on days when you're not feeling particularly grateful.

My prayer is that you'll use this book to deepen your love for God and for others. So let's get started with a prayer:

> *Father, I come to You now and ask that You use this book to guide me into a deeper, more intimate love relationship with You—one of obedience and extreme faithfulness. And Lord, I pray that my beauty would not merely be that of outer adornment but also one that reflects my inner qualities—in particular, who I am, the daughter of the King of kings and Lord of lords. I ask that I would mirror my beauty from the inside out and be a supermodel for You. In Jesus' name...amen.*

Just as water mirrors your face, so
your face mirrors your heart.

—Proverbs 27:19

101 MakeOver Minutes

MakeOver Minute #1
SAY "CHEESE!"

One day my husband and I were strolling the streets of New York City, when a billboard caught my eye. It read, "More people will do a double take when they see a smile than when they see a brand-new luxury automobile roll off the showroom floor...so SMILE!"

The thought intrigued me, so I decided to give it a try. I walked arm in arm with my husband, smiling broadly all the way, and you know what? It was true! People *did* take a second look. In fact, many even smiled back. It was great! I realized then and there that a smile is the best—not to mention the most inexpensive—way to improve your looks on the outside while at the same time making you feel better on the inside. A smile is a blessing for both the one who gives *and* the one who receives it.

In the book of Numbers, God smiled on the people of Israel and gave them His blessing of peace as they traveled in the wilderness. His smile was a source of support. Could *your* smile likewise be a source of encouragement, peace, or comfort to someone today? Go ahead—give it a try. Smile, and a grin just might be given back to you!

Go out into the world uncorrupted, a breath of fresh air in this squalid and polluted society. Provide people with a glimpse of good living and of the living God. Carry the light-giving Message into the night.
—Philippians 2:15

May the LORD smile on you and be gracious to you.
May the LORD show you his favor and give you his peace.
—Numbers 6:25-26 NLT

Prayer and Praise / Thankful Thoughts: _____

_____

_____

_____

Without a doubt, a beautiful smile can be one of your most attractive features. A radiant smile gets you noticed wherever you go and can even be an icebreaker in social settings. Making the most of it is a must! Take care of your smile and it will serve you well.

- **Brush:** Brushing at least twice a day is a vital part of proper dental hygiene. Dentists recommend that you use a soft-bristled brush along with your favorite toothpaste and brush your teeth for at least two minutes. Even before baking-soda toothpaste was available, my mother encouraged me to sprinkle baking soda over my regular toothpaste. I still follow that practice, and my teeth are shiny-bright. To brush effectively, place the brush at a 45-degree angle and use gentle, tooth-wide strokes in a back-and-forth and up-and-down motion. Don't forget to brush your tongue to remove excess bacteria and freshen your breath. Also, remember to get a new toothbrush at least every two months—and always after a sickness such as a cold or the flu.

- **Floss:** Don't forget to floss! Flossing is the most effective way to remove plaque build-up, and fight gum disease. Brushing only reaches the outer portions of your teeth but flossing gets between your teeth, allowing the entire tooth to be cleaned.

- **Rinse:** Once you've brushed and flossed, it's time to rinse. Rinsing with mouthwash prevents bacteria buildup and keeps your breath smelling sweet.

- **Checkup:** Get a regular dental cleaning and checkup every six months. These will help keep your gums and teeth healthy as well as detect any problems such as gum disease, oral cancer, or cavities. During your cleaning, a dental hygienist can remove most stains and polish your teeth to a beautiful shine. You will love the look and feel as you walk away with a beautiful smile.

- **Whitening:** It used to be that you had to spend big bucks at the dentist to whiten your teeth. Not anymore! Now, there are a variety of at-home tooth-whitening treatments that work quite well—and at a fraction of the cost.

A smile speaks all languages to all generations, so brush, floss, and rinse—and show off your glamorous grin!

MakeOver Minute #2
LOOKING GOOD FROM THE INSIDE OUT

Recently I conducted a confidential survey in which I asked a group of gals to answer this question: *If you could change one thing about yourself, what would it be?*

Gal #1 answered, "If there was one thing I could change about myself, it would be my wide hips."

Later, I asked the same group a second question: *If you could change one thing about each gal in this group, what would it be?*

Here are several comments that represented the general response to how the women in the group would change Gal #1:

"If there were one thing I could change about her, it would be her negative attitude toward herself—in particular, the way she puts herself down."

"I'd change her critical mind-set."

This survey and others like it prove what I've suspected all along. When we think about changing ourselves, we think of our outward appearance. When those who know us are asked about changing us, they typically mention our inner qualities rather than our outer features.

So although outer makeovers are great, a successful transformation must begin on the inside. Even though strangers or casual acquaintances can form an opinion of you based on what they see on the outside, those who know you best evaluate you by what lies beneath the surface. Who you are on the inside is what really counts in the long run. This is especially true where God is concerned.

For *real* change to take place, you must let God transform who you are on the inside by asking Jesus to be your Savior and making Him Lord of your life. Your outward appearance should reflect who you are in relationship to Jesus Christ.

So, if you could change one thing about yourself, what would it be?

> *God sees not as man sees, for man looks at the outward appearance, but the LORD looks at the heart.*
>
> —1 Samuel 16:7 NASB

_____

_____

_____

Glamour is more than skin-deep. The key to unlocking your inner beauty starts on the inside—beauty balanced by brilliance. For this reason, it's important to never stop learning. Give your brain an assignment. Make learning a priority. It could be anything from reading a book to taking a class to visiting an art gallery. Or perhaps it's a new business endeavor, a change in career, or a brand-new leisure activity. Whatever it is, find something you are interested in and explore it.

Have you ever said to yourself, *I'd like to try that sometime?* My sister-in-law, who has quite an adventurous spirit, tried hot-air ballooning last year, and moved on to hang-gliding lessons this year. She is forever trying new things, and she doesn't allow fear to stop her. Instead, she enlists encouragement, studies up, and gives it a try.

What is holding you back? Time? Resources? Fear? Whatever it is, get a grip, and try something new for a change.

- **Time:** Even if you don't have a lot of time to spare, devoting just a few moments a day to learning about your new interest will prepare you to pursue it when time allows.

- **Resources:** Granted, some undertakings can be a little pricey. Renting equipment, however, is fairly inexpensive. Another option is buying secondhand. You are better off in case you end up not liking whatever it is you are experimenting with.

- **Encouragement:** Enlist support from others. Find two or three people to be your cheerleaders. Turn to them when you feel afraid, frustrated, reluctant, or anxious about your endeavor.

- **Education:** Get the training you need to accomplish your objective. Whether it's a new hobby or a big career move, taking classes or attending conferences does wonders for your future.

Balance your outer beauty with inner brilliance. Make time to learn something new, and remember—you won't know if you don't try.

MakeOver Minute #3
EVERYTHING IN MODERATION

Moderation is the key when it comes to any diet plan. Anything taken to excess can hurt rather than help in the long run.

In order to appreciate moderation you must first understand what an actual diet is and what it isn't. Usually, we think of a diet as something we are participating in for a set amount of time in order to achieve a certain amount of weight loss. But in reality, a diet is a way of life. Your diet is what you put into your body day in and day out.

Many diet plans fail because we think that once we lose the weight, we can also lose our self-control and go back to our former way of eating. In actuality, a diet does not start with what you eat. It instead begins with how you think about food. It all comes down to intake and output. What you take in calorie-wise must be less than or equal to what you burn in order to maintain or lose weight.

Diets are not the only thing that must be practiced in moderation. Exercise, work, and hobbies all must be viewed in balance. When anything becomes an obsession to the point where we are stuffing ourselves with *it* rather than with *God,* it becomes a sin. God wants us to be consumed with Him and nothing else. But He doesn't want us to keep Him all to ourselves. He wants us to first love Him with all our heart, soul, mind, and strength, and then He wants us to share that love with others (see Mark 12:30-31). In all of life, we must balance what we take in with what we put out.

> *Moderation is better than muscle, self-control better than political power.*
>
> —Proverbs 16:32

Prayer and Praise / Thankful Thoughts: _____

_____

_____

_____

Moderation is key to overcoming burnout. Too much of a good thing is too much of a good thing! When you fall into an all-or-nothing thinking pattern, you set yourself up for failure. Dieting is a prime example of this. Statistics show that when people fall off the wagon, they rarely get back on. In some instances, the opposite is true. People become so fixated on their goal that nothing else matters. They become so single-minded that their obsession consumes them day in and day out.

Taking anything to an extreme—diet, exercise, work, rest, or play—is not healthy. You need balance in order to be successful in life. Put things into perspective by striving to be reasonable, flexible, and consistent.

- **Be reasonable.** Success does not always happen without failure, but an endeavor will never be successful without some element of determination. The original *Chicken Soup for the Soul* book is a prime example of this. The manuscript was rejected 140 times before it was finally published, and now it and the subsequent books are a huge success.

- **Be flexible.** Life never proceeds without some type of detour, so don't let one stop you. Things rarely work out as planned. Just recently, I was on my way to Connecticut and came across a roadblock with a detour sign. I had to travel in a roundabout direction, but I did eventually reach my destination. Life is like that. Sometimes we have to "go with the flow" and take the good with the bad before we reach our goal.

- **Be consistent.** Slow and steady stays the course. Take things day by day, learning to manage the short term in order to reach the long-term goal. I remember when my husband and I were saving to buy our first home. We scrimped on things we could do without so we could put extra money aside. We tried to avoid being shortsighted in order to have what we really wanted. It took consistency, but after a few years we finally saved enough and became proud homeowners.

What areas in your life need balance? No matter what they are, take the moderate approach. Be reasonable, flexible, and consistent, and positive results will be sure to follow.

MakeOver Minute #4
SLOUGH IT OFF

About every four to six weeks, new skin emerges from beneath the surface, sloughing off the old skin as it works its way to the top. Exfoliating the skin advances the process by helping to remove the old skin cells so the newer ones come into view. Once the dead skin cells are removed, the newer, healthier cells make the skin's surface appear smooth and radiant.

Did you know that this same principle can apply to our spiritual lives as well? When you ask Jesus into your life, you become a new person. Like exfoliating, as you slough off the old way of life, the radiant new you will shine through in all you say and do.

> *Your body will always be dead because of sin. But if Christ is in you, then the Spirit gives you life, because Christ made you right with God.*
>
> —Romans 8:10 NCV

Is there anything in your life you need to bring to the surface and confess to God? You can always talk to Him to rid yourself of sin and start fresh and anew. Out with old sin—and in with a new way of life!

> *If anyone is in Christ, he is a new creation; the old has gone, the new has come!*
>
> —2 Corinthians 5:17 NIV

Prayer and Praise / Thankful Thoughts: _____

_____

_____

_____

Exfoliants, or facial scrubs, are cleansers specially formulated to remove dead skin cells from the skin's surface and expose fresh, healthy new skin. Old layers of surface skin clog your pores, trapping dirt and sweat and making your skin much more susceptible to blemishes. Exfoliating your face two to three times a week gives you the same glowing results as an expensive facial.

There are two basic types of exfoliants on the market—chemical polishers and manual scrubs. Chemical polishers contain alpha hydroxyl acids (AHAs) that remove dead skin cells. Manual scrubs are made up of fine, gritty substances that are manually worked into the skin to produce the same results. Using your fingertips, gently massage the product into your already dampened skin in a circular motion. This will gently slough off old cells without irritating your skin. Rinse well by splashing water over your face several times until you no longer feel any residue on your skin's surface. Gently blot dry. Follow up with toner, which will remove any leftover traces of exfoliant, then apply moisturizer. (Never use an exfoliant on the delicate skin around your eyes.)

- **Dry skin:** Use a gentle exfoliating scrub to loosen dry skin cells and slough off flaky dead skin. Be careful not to pull, stretch, or irritate sensitive dry skin.

- **Normal skin:** Exfoliating masks are great for normal skin types. Gently massage the mask in with your fingertips, leaving it on for the designated period of time, and rinse off.

- **Combination skin:** Use exfoliating scrubs, polishers, or masks for normal to oily skin types.

- **Oily skin:** Use a water-based or medicated exfoliant to combat oily shine and blemishes. Do not use on severe acne, and always avoid harsh scrubbing that could open up blemishes and spread bacteria.

For centuries, women have known that nature's best exfoliant is oatmeal. Try this recipe for smoother, fresher skin:

1 cup oatmeal
1 15-inch-by-15-inch piece of cheesecloth
1 rubber band

Put oatmeal in cheesecloth and gather ends, tying them off with the rubber band. Dip bag in water and wring out excess moisture. Rub over face in a circular motion, avoiding the eye area. This will rid your skin of dead cells and loosen blackheads. Next, undo the rubber band and apply the wet oatmeal directly to your face. Lean back and relax, leaving the oatmeal on your face for five minutes before rinsing well with warm water. Finish up with your favorite moisturizer.

MakeOver Minute #5
ATTITUDE CHECK

Did you know there's one fashion accessory available to anyone and everyone at absolutely no cost? It's your own individual attitude! The clothes you wear, the color of your hair, and the condition of your skin cannot compare to the knockout effect of a positive attitude.

Chuck Swindoll once said,

> The remarkable thing is, we have a choice every day regarding the attitude we will embrace for that day. We cannot change our past... we cannot change the fact that people will act in a certain way. We cannot change the inevitable. The only thing we can do is play on the one string we have, and that is our attitude...I am convinced that life is 10% what happens to me and 90% how I react to it. And so it is with you...you are in charge of your attitude.

The Bible says we are to have the attitude of Christ, and the attitude Jesus displayed was one of love and forgiveness. This is exactly what God expects from us:

> *You must clothe yourselves with tenderhearted mercy, kindness, humility, gentleness, and patience. You must make allowance for each other's faults and forgive the person who offends you. Remember, the Lord forgave you, so you must forgive others. And the most important piece of clothing you must wear is love.*
>
> —Colossians 3:12-14 NLT

> *May God, who gives this patience and encouragement, help you live in complete harmony with each other—each with the attitude of Christ Jesus toward the other.*
>
> —Romans 15:5 NLT

Prayer and Praise / Thankful Thoughts: _____
_____
_____
_____

Style is not only about makeup, hair, and clothing. It's also about the attitude in which you present yourself. A put-together attitude sets you apart, giving you the edge over up-to-the-minute fashion and keeping you in tip-top style.

How do you feel when you put on a drop-dead gorgeous outfit for the first time? I don't know about you, but new clothes make me feel great! They give me an upbeat, I'm-ready-to-take-on-the-world kind of attitude. However, I find my attitude to be much like my clothing—it changes all the time.

Circumstances often cause negative attitudes, but wouldn't it be great if the opposite were true and a positive attitude influenced our circumstances? You have the power to change your own attitude *and* actions, which is a much more practical approach than hoping your external circumstances will be perfect. Instead of becoming increasingly overwhelmed by circumstances, optimistically work through them.

Every day you have a choice—to be in a good mood or to be in a bad mood. Each time something bad happens, you can choose to be a victim or choose to act objectively and learn from it. When someone else tries to bring you down by arguing and complaining, you can choose to receive it or you can choose to refute it with a positive interpretation. It's up to you to choose the negative or the positive side of life. Every situation is an opportunity to accentuate the positive!

Your attitude is driven by your love for God, which directly relates to how you love others. A loving and forgiving approach promotes a winning attitude, and although it can be difficult to practice in all situations, a positive attitude accessorized with prayer and determination leads to a successful outlook. Your attitude is your choice. No one else can control it, and only you can allow anyone or anything to affect it. It's yours to do with what you want. Change your attitude and change your perspective. How will you wear yours today?

Remember, being beautiful is a process. It all starts with your attitude, which directly affects your perception, both in the way you view life and in the way others view you. Design your attitude after the Designer of the universe and you'll never go out of style!

MakeOver Minute #6
HAIR WE GO AGAIN

Want a makeover without breaking the bank? A brand-new haircut and color is the quickest, most inexpensive way to get a total makeover. Smart, sassy, short, or straight, your lovely locks can give you great new style!

Have you ever gone to the hair salon with a cut or color in mind that looked attractive on someone else but, once it was on you, looked hideous? I have! Long before I understood face shape, hair texture, and skin tone, I tried to pull off a permed, buttery-blond bob. The color made my skin look sallow, and the frizzy curls made my face look swollen. It made me feel awful about myself. My self-esteem plummeted as I imagined people laughing behind my back. I couldn't wait for my hair to grow out so I could have it corrected.

My self-worth was definitely challenged by this hairstyle. Sound silly? Ridiculous or not, we all fear rejection at some point. When our acceptance is threatened by anything, we start to feel insecure. But there's good news! God accepts, values, and esteems us—even on bad hair days. He loves us no matter what. His love and care are unconditional. When you accept Jesus as your Savior, you become the bride of Christ. Just as the wedding vows state, "for better or for worse, for richer or for poor, in sickness and in health...on good hair days and bad [my own addition]." God loves you all the time! Even when most of the world gives up on a person, God is there—loving, caring, and watching over His own. He esteems you and values you all the days of your life.

I will be your God throughout your lifetime—until your hair is white with age. I made you, and I will care for you. I will carry you along and save you.

—Isaiah 46:4 NLT

Prayer and Praise / Thankful Thoughts: _____

_____

_____

_____

Need a new do? It doesn't matter whether you've been stuck in a hair rut or just need a quick change. You can save yourself from hair-raising results by following a few simple hair-do's.

First, picture it! A picture is worth a thousand words. Having a photograph of what you want the stylist to accomplish will help eliminate hair bloopers. Flip through magazines for hairstyle and color choices. When you find something that appeals to you, ask yourself and the stylist these questions:

- Does the cut suit the shape of my face?

- Will it work with the texture of my hair?

- How easily will I be able to re-create the style at home?

- Will I need any special styling tools or products?

- Is the color right for my skin tone?

- How often will the color need to be touched up?

Second, have stylist savvy! Picking a quality hair stylist or colorist can be difficult at best if you don't know what to look for. However, following these steps will help you in your quest:

- If you see someone with great hair, ask for the name of her salon and stylist.

- Find a stylist who is Redken-certified. These stylists have to stay current on up-to-the-minute trends in the hair industry in order to maintain their certification.

Remember, if you do get your hair done and you are unhappy with it for any reason, be sure and let the hairdresser know. He or she should fix it to your satisfaction at no extra charge. If you're not sure about your new look because it's a drastic change, give it a few days before asking to have it redone.

MakeOver Minute #7
BATHING BEAUTY

Taking a bubble bath by candlelight while listening to soft music can be an excellent way to relieve stress, ease depression, and relax yourself before bedtime. Bath time also gives you a quiet moment to pray, meditate, and listen to God.

I don't know what it is about soaking in a hot, steamy, fragrant bath, but somehow it always seems to alleviate stress and wash my worries down the drain with the pull of the plug. A bath relieves, refreshes, and renews my soul through the most difficult of times.

Throughout the Bible, water was used to revitalize and bring new life to both men and women. Starting with Noah, God sent rain to purge the earth and cleanse it from sin. We also find in the Pentateuch that spiritual cleansing was necessary to preserve the law. In the New Testament, Jesus identifies Himself as Living Water: "The water that I shall give him will become in him a fountain of water springing up into everlasting life" (John 4). Water symbolically heals, restores, and gives life.

Here are some of my favorite verses to soak up as I bathe:

- **Relax:** "Showing respect to the LORD brings true life—if you do it, you can relax without fear of danger" (Proverbs 19:23 CEV).

- **Reflect:** "I will study your commandments and reflect on your ways" (Psalm 119:15 NLT).

- **Renew:** "There must be a spiritual renewal of your thoughts and attitudes" (Ephesians 4:23 NLT).

- **Refresh:** "Repent and return, so that your sins may be wiped away, in order that times of refreshing may come from the presence of the Lord" (Acts 3:19 NASB).

- **Restore:** "Restore to me the joy of Your salvation, and uphold me by Your generous Spirit" (Psalm 51:12 NKJV).

- **Relieve:** "Relieve the troubles of my heart, and bring me out of my distress" (Psalm 25:17 NRS).

...Casting all your anxiety on Him because He cares for you.

—1 Peter 5:7 NASB

Give your worries to the LORD, and He will take care of you. He will never let good people down.

—Psalm 55:22 NCV

Prayer and Praise / Thankful Thoughts: _____

_____

_____

_____

- This is my favorite recipe for Lavender Bath Salts:

    2 cups Epsom salts
    1 cup sea salt
    1/2 cup nonfat powdered milk
    1 cup old-fashioned oatmeal, ground to a fine powder in a food
        processor
    20 drops lavender essential oil

- In a large bowl, mix together by hand all dry ingredients. Add the lavender essential oil five drops at a time, thoroughly mixing after each addition. After all 20 drops have been added, continue to mix until all oil is well distributed and absorbed. Store in an airtight container. Use one-half to one cup of salts per bath, depending on the size of your tub.

- Chamomile tea is not just for drinking! After a hard day, toss a couple of tea bags into a warm bath and relax. Within a half-hour, stress is relieved, senses are soothed, and you'll feel great.

- Another great way to unwind is by using aromatherapy. To make my Vanilla Extract Aromatherapy, add one-quarter to one-third cup of pure vanilla extract to a warm bath. The aroma of vanilla can help you relax and de-stress.

MakeOver Minute #8
ACCENTUATE THE POSITIVE

Playing up your best qualities draws attention away from your less-than-flattering features. If you have great hair but wide hips, wear a hairstyle that flatters your face shape and draws the eye up and away from your problem area. Enhancing your finer features distracts from your more challenging areas.

Of course, there are things you can change about yourself and those you cannot. For instance, you can control a weight problem, but you cannot change the shape of your nose without cosmetic surgery. You can remove unwanted facial hair, but you can't make yourself any taller.

The same is true of who we are and how we behave spiritually. There are things we can do to increase our faith, and there are natural things that cannot be changed. The fact is, we will always sin here on earth. Yet there are things we can do to downplay our sinful nature and become more Christlike. Work on the things you can change by accentuating the positive to eliminate the negative. Read and apply Scripture (Isaiah 55:11), pray (Philippians 4:6), avoid temptation (Matthew 26:41), and rely on the Holy Spirit for guidance (Galatians 5:16). As you grow in your faith, your old way of living will be overshadowed by your new way of life. Soon the good will outweigh the bad as you cultivate a positive outlook that offers hope to those around you.

Since, then, we do not have the excuse of ignorance, everything—and I do mean everything—connected with that old way of life has to go. It's rotten through and through. Get rid of it! And then take on an entirely new way of life—a God-fashioned life, a life renewed from the inside.

—Ephesians 4:22-23

Prayer and Praise / Thankful Thoughts: _____

_____

_____

_____

Each one of us has things we like about ourselves and things we do not. Some we can't change, but there are three basic qualities that everyone can improve upon—your smile, your posture, and your overall hygiene.

Taking care of your mouth, teeth, and gums prevents bad breath, tooth decay, and gum disease. Good dental hygiene promotes a healthy smile as well as fresh breath. If your teeth are dingy, have them whitened. Nothing improves a smile and makes you look younger like whiter, brighter teeth.

Perfect posture can make you appear taller and slimmer while giving you an air of self-assuredness. Good posture begins by pulling your abdominal muscles in and stretching your neck as though a string is pulling your head toward the ceiling. Next, straighten your shoulders by rotating your arms backward, gently pressing them down. Now, pull your shoulder blades toward your spine and press them down toward your waistline. Finally, relax your arms next to your side and finish with a deep, cleansing breath.

My grandma used to say, "Cleanliness is next to godliness." Words to live by, for sure! With the abundance of personal cleaning products on the market, there is little excuse for poor hygiene. Take pride in yourself by bathing, washing, and combing your hair, eliminating body odor (including stinky feet), and wearing clean, tidy clothing.

These are the basic things we can do to improve ourselves as well as enhance our positive qualities. What is *your* best feature? How can you accentuate it?

MakeOver Minute #9
OUT WITH THE OLD, IN WITH THE NEW

We've heard it said again and again: *out with the old, in with the new.* But how many of us truly live by this saying? Typically, our standard of living has evolved into "in with the new, and keep the old too." This is one reason we think we need bigger homes along with additional storage facilities to house our things. It doesn't matter if we're clearing out the makeup drawer, the garage, or the closet of our heart—we avoid dealing with stuff because it's hard work. The fact is, it's much easier to be a pack rat both externally and internally rather than face the alternative.

Luke chapter 3 paints a vivid picture of the very issue of cleaning out. Once you ask Jesus into your life, your body has a new purpose: "Don't you know that your body is the temple of the Holy Spirit, who lives in you and was given to you by God?" (1 Corinthians 6:19 NLT).

It's like selling your house to someone without cleaning it out before the new residents move in. They take possession and immediately have to start clearing a path so they can reside (uncomfortably, I might add) as they work on getting rid of your junk. That's what the Holy Spirit does in each one of us. He moves in and starts cleaning house. His job is to help you clean up your act by convicting you of your old, sinful habits.

The problem is, many of us are attached to our old way of life and don't want to let go of the sin with which we've become emotionally comfortable. We want it both ways, and then we wonder why our lives are a mess. The fact is, once you receive Jesus, your contaminated old self has expired. You now house the Holy Spirit of God. Doesn't He merit a good, old-fashioned spring cleaning of the heart—the kind that deals with everything and makes a clean sweep? It's time—out with the old, and in with a new way of life!

The Holy spirit [will be] within you, changing you from the inside out. He's going to clean house—make a clean sweep of your lives. He'll place everything true in its proper place before God; everything false he'll put out with the trash to be burned.

—Luke 3:16-17

When was the last time you sorted through your cosmetics and tossed out the old stuff? I know it's hard to throw away something that hasn't been used up, but for safety's sake it's time to clean out.

Generally, cosmetics are formulated and packaged for a shelf life of one to three years. However, once the product has been opened and exposed to sunlight and air pollutants, it breaks down much more quickly and will deteriorate well before the expiration date. This is especially true of eye makeup. Once it becomes contaminated, you run the risk of developing an eye infection. Below is a list of how long cosmetic products usually last. (If the item in question breaks down or develops a smell, discard it immediately.)

- skin-care products (cleansers, gels, and creams): 12 months
- concealer: 12 months
- foundation: 12 months for water-based; 18 months for oil-based
- compact or loose powder: 24 months
- blush: 12 months
- eye shadow: 24 to 36 months
- eyeliner pencil: 36 months
- liquid eyeliner: 6 months
- mascara: 3 to 4 months
- lip-liner pencil: 36 months
- lip color: 12 to 24 months
- nail polish: 18 to 24 months

As you clean out, get rid of things you don't use—such as the mood lipstick that seemed like a good idea at the time—and products that are the wrong color for your skin tone or the wrong formula for your skin type. Cleaning out always leaves me with a sense of accomplishment. It doesn't matter whether I'm cleaning out my makeup drawer or digging a little deeper into the drawer of my heart. A fresh start always does wonders for who I am on the outside *and* on the inside.

MakeOver Minute #10
THE GOLDEN RULE OF THUMB

Do you do for others what you want them to do for you, or do you instead give them what they deserve? Unfortunately, I think all too often we tend to choose the second option. We want to treat others exactly how we've been treated. Although that might seem fair, is it, really? Isn't God the one who will repay as He sees fit?

> *My friends, do not try to punish others when they wrong you, but wait for God to punish them with his anger. It is written: "I will punish those who do wrong; I will repay them," says the Lord.*
> —Romans 12:19 NCV

Now, let's look at the flip side of the situation. Are you not *outrageously* overjoyed God does not give you what you deserve? I am! According to Romans 6:23, "the wages of sin is death"—spiritual death, the kind of death that separates you from God for all eternity. What we deserve is never-ending damnation, but God saw fit to save us despite what we have earned.

And what about God? What does *He* deserve? Do you treat Him the way you want Him to treat you? Do you ask for blessings though you have backslidden? Do you expect God's best although you don't give yours? These are questions you need to ask yourself before you decide what's best for someone else.

God called you to love Him and others unconditionally, in both good times and bad. The best way you can display that love is by following the Golden Rule: "Just as you want others to do for you, do the same for them" (HCS).

Remember, you are openly expressing your love for God when you serve others without expecting anything in return (see Matthew 25:34-45).

> *Treat others the same way you want them to treat you.*
> —Luke 6:31 NASB

Prayer and Praise / Thankful Thoughts: _____

_____

_____

_____

Do unto others as you would have them do unto you. This verse (Luke 6:31) is known as the Golden Rule. This to-the-point instruction is commonly taught prior to kindergarten, yet we often grow up without learning how to put it into practice. Why? Because even though it sounds simple, it happens to be one of those things that's a lot easier said than done.

The Golden Rule is an age-old solution to one of life's greatest problems—self-centeredness. Just think how peaceful the world would be if we took the focus off ourselves and placed it on those around us. What if you treated others the way you would like to be treated? What if each of us practiced acts of kindness without expecting anything in return? Hmm...giving without getting? Is that possible? Yes, it is! The first thing to do is to get over yourself and move past your number-one problem—me, myself and I. *Me* has an attitude of self-centeredness. *Myself* wants everything "her way or the highway." And *I* is an egomaniac.

In my own little world, it's all about me! My definition of the Golden Rule reads, "Treat me the way I want to be treated—period!" Girls, it's true. Many of us have "I" problems, but it's time we take our eyes off ourselves and look around to see who it is we could treat better. Who can you encourage today—a family member, a friend, a co-worker, the harried mother with her three children standing in line at the supermarket? Remember, it's not about what you *get*, but what you *give* of yourself that makes the rule golden.

MakeOver Minute #11
A "SONNY" DISPOSITION

I once passed a church billboard that read, "Exposure to the Son can save you from burning." Wow—what truth! Those who enter into a relationship with Jesus Christ are saved from an eternity of burning in hell.

I remember one particular summer day I spent on the beach. I was studying for a college exam, not realizing my sunblock had lost its effectiveness. That evening, my sunburn became more and more evident as my skin got redder and the pain intensified. The only relief I found was sitting in a tub of cool water, and even that was only temporary. This reminds me of Luke 16:24, where the rich man cries out from hell, "Father Abraham! Take pity on me, and send Lazarus to dip his finger in some water and cool off my tongue, because I am in great pain in this fire!" (GNT).

The sunburn I suffered from healed eventually, but in hell, there is no healing, no help, and no end to the eternity of extreme suffering (see Matthew 13). There is, though, a "Sonblock" that will save you.

Praise God for His Son, Jesus, who came to prevent us from getting burned and to give us an eternity filled with Sonlight. God provides us with a Son Protection Factor (SPF) that gives 100 percent coverage. All you have to do is apply it once and you're good to go forever. Have you applied yours? If not, why not do it right now?

Dear Jesus,

Thank You for loving me and dying on the cross for my sins. I need You, and I ask that You to come into my life and save me. Please help me to know and love You better every day. In Jesus' Name, Amen.

There will be no night there—no need for lamps or sun—for the Lord God will shine on them. And they will reign forever and ever.

—Revelation 22:5 NLT

Prayer and Praise / Thankful Thoughts: _____

_____

_____

Unprotected exposure to the sun's ultraviolet rays—UVA or UVB—produces 90 percent of the symptoms related to skin cancer and premature skin aging, such as wrinkles and age spots. In order to avoid the dangers of the sun, it is important to use a sunscreen with a SPF (Sun Protection Factor) of 15 or higher. For maximum protection, you must apply it correctly. Below are some sun-savvy steps to help your skin look "sunsational" throughout your life:

- Use a waterproof sunblock if you will be sweating or swimming.
- Use specially formulated sunscreen on your face.
- Use a water-based sunscreen if you have oily skin or are prone to acne.
- Be aware of your sunscreen's expiration date. Ingredients can break down over time and lose their effectiveness.
- Apply sunscreen 30 minutes prior to going out into the sun so that it has time to absorb into your skin. Then, just before you go out, apply a second coat.
- Do not skimp on sunscreen. Always apply a generous amount to ensure complete coverage.
- Do not forget your ears, your neck, the backs of your knees, and the tops of your feet.
- Be careful not to get sunscreen in your eyes.
- Apply sunscreen every two hours, and more often than that if you are exercising or swimming.
- Apply sunscreen in addition to wearing a hat or protective clothing.
- Do not forget to apply sunscreen on cloudy or overcast days.
- Drink plenty of water.

Even if you use foundation that contains an SPF, still apply sunscreen first. Most foundations contain only an SPF 8, and an SPF 15 is needed for optimum benefit. Also, keep in mind that not only will sunscreen protect from sun damage, it will help keep your skin moisturized all over.

MakeOver Minute #12
IF THE SHOE FITS...

Shoes come in every color, for every season, for all occasions—functional flats, sexy stilettos, comfy cross trainers, sassy sandals, perfect pumps. Shoes are available to accomplish any undertaking, whether it's going to the gym or spending a day at the beach. The proper foot attire is an essential part of our wardrobe. In fact, it's so important that God mentions it in the Bible.

Ephesians 6:15 illustrates the most precious and priceless pair of shoes that anyone can possess, "the good news shoes of peace," which have a life-changing fit. Once you receive Christ, you possess extraordinary peace: "The peace of God, which surpasses all understanding, will guard your hearts and your minds in Christ Jesus" (Philippians 4:7 NRS). The question is, do you rely on this peace? We live in a desperate world full of unrest, depression, hardship, problems, and disaster, but as a Christian you can offer hope and peace in the midst of turmoil.

In Ephesians 6, God teaches us how to dress for success, which includes wearing the shoes of peace. These shoes are specifically designed to bring calm in the midst of chaos. You'll know if you have them on by the way you react to difficult situations. Do you look up for help or sink down into depression? Do you trust God to walk you through it, or do you run out of control? Do you rely on God to see you through, or do you try other things such as money, addictions, or impulsive relationships? How you respond to circumstances beyond your control shows others your faith in God. Is it real? Do you live it, or do you just talk a good talk? It's not until you put feet to your faith that your hope in God becomes the "gospel of peace" (Romans 10:15) that others long to know.

Having been justified by faith, we have peace with God through our Lord Jesus Christ.

—Romans 5:1 NKJV

Your desire to tell the good news about peace should be like shoes on your feet.

—Ephesians 6:15 CEV

_____

_____

_____

> When a woman gets dressed to kill, her feet are usually her first victims.
>
> —Author unknown

It might surprise you to know that the majority of foot problems in women stem from wearing the wrong size, shape, and style of shoes. Apparently, we base our decisions more on how shoes look than how they feel. I'll have to confess that I'm guilty of this very thing. In the past, I've found shoes on the clearance rack that were a half-size too small but bought them anyway, thinking I'd stretch them out. However, my feet ended up suffering the consequences until I finally got rid of the shoes.

So be shoe-smart. Do your feet a favor and purchase shoes that look good, feel comfortable, and fit right from the start. You can take the guesswork out of shoe sizing by having an expert measure your feet. This free service is available at most major department stores, whether or not you make a purchase.

It's wise to have your feet measured later in the day when they are tired and swollen. This will help you avoid buying shoes that are stylish yet uncomfortable.

Make sure you have the length and width of each foot measured. It is common to have one foot that is larger than the other. In this case, buy shoes based on the size of your larger foot.

If you follow this advice and still feel like you are getting blisters, apply petroleum jelly to the parts of your feet that are rubbing against your shoes. This helps to reduce the friction. If you do develop a blister, clean and dry the spot, then apply an antibiotic ointment with a cotton swab. Next, cover the blister with a Band-Aid. Apply petroleum jelly to the Band-Aid, which will help keep it from rubbing off.

MakeOver Minute #13
GOING SOLO

One of the most cherished lessons I learned growing up was the need to go solo with God. At camp, we would set aside a three-hour block of time to spend alone with God. We could sit by the lake, go into the woods, or find a quiet spot around the camp to read the Bible, pray, listen, and journal.

At first, three hours seemed like an eternity, but as the demands of the world faded away and I allowed myself to bask in God's love, three hours was hardly enough. As it turned out, I didn't want the time to be up. This experience alone with God made me ready to face whatever challenges there were with a revitalized strength and vigor I had previously been missing.

Alone time with God is a vital part of the Christian life. It allows us to mature, persevere, and flourish in our faith. It also gives us time to meditate on His Word and listen as He speaks.

> *I will meditate on Your precepts, and contemplate Your ways.*
> —Psalm 119:15 NKJV

Can you find a quiet place of solitude today? Spend some much-needed alone time with the One who loves, values, and cares for you more than anyone or anything else. Remember, when you go solo with God, you are never alone.

> *Here's what I want you to do: find a quiet, secluded place so you won't be tempted to role-play before God. Just be there as simply and honestly as you can manage. The focus will shift from you to God, and you will begin to sense his grace.*
> —Matthew 6:6 CEV

Prayer and Praise / Thankful Thoughts: _____

_____

_____

_____

Gals, alone time is essential to your overall well-being. As a busy woman, if I let myself down, I will be of little or no value to those who need me the most—my heavenly Father, my husband, my children, my extended family, and my friends. We practice what we believe to be self-denial, thinking this will make us heroically humble. But in reality, it hinders our helpfulness.

Well, it's time for you to get a new lease on life. I want to encourage you to develop a "me first" attitude. Now, please don't misunderstand my definition of "me first." I do *not* characterize "me first" as self-centeredness, but instead a means of developing your self-confidence—the kind that comes from improving who you are from the inside out. Here are some of my favorite "me first" methods to help refresh, relax, and revitalize you:

- Spend time at a spa for a facial, manicure, pedicure, or massage.
- Steep a spot of tea in a porcelain teapot, then serve it up to yourself in a elegant china teacup with saucer.
- Take an art class, music lesson, or writing course, or join a book club.
- Go for a walk, taking time to get a breath of fresh air and a little exercise too.
- Take a bubble bath by candlelight.
- Spend a moment counting your blessings. Write them down so that next time you're feeling blue, you can refer to the list as a source of encouragement.
- End your day by journaling. Write down your reflections from the day and at least one thing for which you are thankful.
- Unplug and unwind by turning off your cell phone, fax, pager, computer, and answering machine for at least an hour.
- Take a 20-minute power nap.
- Watch an old "feel good" movie or read a favorite book.

Whatever it is, make time for *you*. Give yourself permission to put your needs first so you are refreshed, recharged, and ready to meet the demands life puts on you. Remember, when you feel better, you look better. And when you look better, you can face the day with a renewed confidence.

MakeOver Minute #14
SIGNATURE SCENT

Our sense of smell helps us identify people, places, and things. For example, I could be blindfolded and still tell you when my mom entered a room or had recently been there by the one and only perfume she always wore. Or I could unknowingly be dropped off at my friends' lemon ranch and tell you exactly where I was just by the unique aroma of the orchards. How about you? Can you tell when there are cinnamon rolls in the oven, or when someone in the neighborhood has chicken on the outdoor grill? Smells inform, warn, and direct us through life.

In 2 Corinthians 2:14-15, we see that God compares those who have a relationship with Him through His Son Jesus to a sweet aroma or fragrance to the lost. In the Old Testament, Aaron and the other priests were anointed with special fragrant oil that was poured over their heads and ran down their faces and into their robes. It permeated their skin, beard, and clothes, making them easy to identify. These were the men chosen by God to inform the people of the law, warn them about the consequences of breaking the commandments, and direct them in the ways and teachings of the one and only true God.

Gals, if you have accepted Jesus as your Savior, God has anointed you. As a Christian, you are marked by His signature scent, and it's your mission to inform, warn, and direct people to God through His Son Jesus Christ. Inform them of the truth (John 14:6), warn them about eternity without Christ (Romans 6:23), and direct them to life in Christ (2 Thessalonians 3:5). When you do these things, they will truly become heaven "scent" (2 Corinthians 2:15).

Thanks be to God, who always leads us in triumph in Christ, and manifests through us the sweet aroma of knowledge of Him in every place. For we are a fragrance of Christ to God among those who are being saved and among those who are perishing.

—2 Corinthians 2:14-15 NASB

_____

_____

_____

Do you have a signature scent, one that you like and that likes you? There are numerous fragrances on the market, but no one fragrance is suitable for every person. I've smelled many nice perfumes on sample cards, but when I actually applied them to my skin, they didn't really smell that great. Finding a scent that works with you instead of against you is the difference between people welcoming or avoiding you. To find a friendly fragrance, try them on one at time, wait for a period of 15 minutes, and then see if they pass the smell test. If you're still not sure, get a second opinion from a loved one.

If you want your scent to last all day, layer it by using a companion shower gel and body lotion. When you shower, exfoliate before you use the shower gel. This will remove dead skin cells and give the shower gel fresh new cells for the scent to permeate. Once you get out of the shower, gently towel dry, then immediately apply the body lotion to moistened skin. Next, apply the fragrance to your pulse points—wrists, décolletage, behind your ears and knees. As an added bonus, spray your hairbrush with perfume before you brush your hair, or add several drops of your favorite fragrance to the rinse water of your hosiery or lingerie.

Our sense of smell affects us on so many levels. Whether pleasant or unpleasant, sensitivity to odors can bring about different feelings. Whenever I smell bacon, it takes me back to my childhood. Just about every morning I woke up to that savory smell wafting from our country kitchen. Old Spice immediately reminds me of a certain uncle, and I'm always reminded of home whenever I smell Yankee Candle's "Home Sweet Home" fragrance, which is what I've used for years in my own house. Have you developed a signature scent for your home, one that will bring family and friends back whenever they smell something similar?

A signature scent is like an autograph. It leaves behind a personal mark, creates memories, and stimulates moods. In fact, long after you step out of a room, your scent can linger, reminding others of your presence. So choose wisely as to what type of scent you want to leave behind.

MakeOver Minute #15
PEOPLE PLEASER

God's Word never tells us what *not* to do without telling what we should be doing instead. In fact, not only do we have the Scripture to guide us, but we also have Jesus' life as a perfect example of how we should live out our faith in Christ.

In Philippians 2:3-5, we can find a set of do's and don'ts to live by. We should be humble, not selfish. We should think of others instead of ourselves instead of living to make a good impression. And we should be interested in others, not simply concerned with our own affairs.

Jesus took a genuine interest in others. First and foremost, He loved unconditionally and listened without condemning, which in turn enabled Him to lead others by grace. Girlfriend, it's the same with you and me. Our aim should be to understand and *then* be understood. There's a saying, "People don't care how much you know until they know how much you care." That's so true! Our goal as sisters in Christ should be to lift hearts and move them to spiritual gladness. Like Jesus, our main objectives ought to be listen, love, and lead others to an everlasting relationship with the Father.

Don't be selfish; don't live to make a good impression on others.
Be humble, thinking of others as better than yourself.
Don't think only about your own affairs, but be interested in others, too, and what they are doing. Your attitude should be the same that Christ Jesus had.
—Philippians 2:3-5 NLT

Prayer and Praise / Thankful Thoughts: _____

_____

_____

_____

Some of the best advice I've ever received is this: People should feel better about themselves having been around you. Too often, the opposite is true. We try to make ourselves feel more important and look better by putting others down. We want to come across secure in who we are, but we usually use this tactic to mask our insecurity. We don't want others to catch on to the fact that we lack self-assurance, so we talk about some other poor unfortunate soul to keep people from scrutinizing us. We use criticism as a means of receiving positive acceptance and approval. Although it may seem to work for a time, people eventually grow tired of it and reject us because of our faultfinding natures.

People are drawn to optimistic individuals who lift up, affirm, and encourage. They're not drawn to pessimists who put down and pass judgment. People like being around individuals who offer hope and make them feel good about themselves. Isn't this true for you? Wouldn't you prefer compliments in place of criticism? Even now, I'm sure you can think of someone you like to be around for this very reason. The good news is, *you* can be that person! You have the power to be an encourager rather than a discourager.

To do this, first think about what you are going to say before you say it. Does it build up or belittle? Next, be aware of the tone in which you say it. Is it sincere or sarcastic? Finally, make a conscious effort to benefit the hearer. Will what you say have a positive effect or a negative impact?

Always choose your words wisely. Make others happy that they made your acquaintance, not sorry they met you. Characterize your presence by offering hope, confidence, and cheer, and you will never be without friends.

It takes a series of steps to get perfectly manicured nails. Likewise, God gives us steps to fully manicured lives in Him and through Him. He gives us everything we need to cleanse, soften, shape, prepare, condition, polish, and shield our lives according to His purpose and plan.

In step one, you *cleanse* your life by receiving Christ as your Savior: "If we confess our sins, He is faithful and righteous to forgive us our sins and to cleanse us from all unrighteousness" (1 John 1:9 NASB).

Step two involves *softening* your disposition. God esteems gentle strength: "Your beauty should consist of your true inner self, the ageless beauty of a gentle and quiet spirit, which is of the greatest value in God's sight" (1 Peter 3:4 GNT).

You *shape* your life after Christ in step three. Jesus is the perfect example of the kind of Christlike life we are to strive for: "God knew what he was doing from the very beginning. He decided from the outset to shape the lives of those who love him along the same lines as the life of his Son. The Son stands first in the line of humanity he restored. We see the original and intended shape of our lives there in him" (Romans 8:29).

For step four, *prepare* yourself with Scripture and prayer to face day-to-day challenges: "Do your best, prepare for the worst—then trust GOD to bring victory" (Proverbs 21:31).

Next comes step five—*conditioning* who you are and all you say and do to honor God. God can use you to glorify Him in your current situation, unless of course you are involved with something that is immoral or unethical: "Brethren, each one is to remain with God in that condition in which he was called" (1 Corinthians 7:24 NASB).

In step six, you *polish* your life and let it shine from the inside out: "Let your light shine before men in such a way that they may see your good works, and glorify your Father who is in heaven" (Matthew 5:16 NASB).

And last comes step seven—*shielding* yourself in the protection of the Lord: "The LORD is my strength and my shield; my heart trusts in Him, and I am helped; therefore my heart exults, and with my song I shall thank Him" (Psalm 28:7 NASB).

In all things, God acts as a buffer to those who love Him and do His will, which will in turn strengthen you and encourage spiritual growth.

> *Close the book on Evil, GOD, but publish your mandate for us.*
> *You get us ready for life: you probe for our soft spots,*
> *you knock off our rough edges.*
>
> —Psalm 7:9

Prayer and Praise / Thankful Thoughts: _____

_____

_____

_____

Did you know that your fingernails are a great way to accessorize any outfit? No matter if you are going to the beach, the office, or a swanky formal affair, perfectly manicured nails add the finishing touch to anything you wear.

These days the nail business has become a hot commodity, with nail joints springing up on every corner. Women—and men too—have become concerned with well-manicured hands. While going to the salon is nice, this luxury can be performed at home at a substantial savings. Follow the directions below to achieve professional salon results at a minimum cost—all in the convenience of your own home.

You'll need the following supplies:

- bowl
- orange stick
- base coat of nail polish
- bubble bath or bath salts
- nail polish or nail lacquer
- denture-cleaning tablet (optional)

- top coat of nail polish
- nailbrush or toothbrush
- buffing cream
- buffer (optional)
- hand lotion
- lip balm (optional)
- nail file or emery board
- acetone-free nail polish remover
- cotton balls

Now you're ready to start. First, *cleanse* your nails by giving your fingers a bubble bath. Put several drops of your favorite bubble bath solution or a sprinkle of bath salts into a bowl and fill with warm water. Soak your fingers for five minutes in the scented water prior to starting your manicure. If your nails are yellow or stained, use a denture-cleaning tablet instead of bubble bath and gently scrub nails with a nailbrush or toothbrush. Dry your hands and nails, then massage in your favorite hand lotion.

Now, *soften* and strengthen your cuticles by applying lip balm to them. Use an orange stick to gently push them back. Never cut your cuticles. They act as a seal to the nail bed and protect against infection. If you have dry, cracked cuticles, apply the lip balm daily to help care for them.

Shape your nails by holding the emery board at a slight angle to the nail, gently filing the nail from the outside corner of the nail to the center. Repeat this process from the opposite corner of the nail. Remember that the shape of your nail should mirror your cuticle shape.

Next, *prepare* your nails to be polished by dousing a cotton ball with nail polish remover and carefully cleaning the lotion and lip balm residue from your nail bed.

Now you're ready to *condition* your nails by applying a base coat. This will also help prevent the nail polish from chipping and peeling.

Polish your nails with two thin coats of nail polish or lacquer.

Then *shield* and protect your freshly painted nails by adding a top coat. If you prefer buffed nails to polished nails, skip the last three steps. Instead, apply a dab of buffing cream to each nail. Next, vigorously buff each nail to a glossy shine by quickly moving the buffer back and forth across your nail from different angles. Buffing nails is good for them—it increases blood flow, which strengthens them and stimulates growth.

MakeOver Minute #17
BEAUTY SLEEP

According to the Bible, a good night's sleep is a gift from God. Contrary to what some may believe, sleep is not a sin unless it is provoked by evil deeds or extreme laziness.

The majority of sleep deprivation is driven by stress—some of which is self-inflicted and some of which is imposed on you—but all of which can be tolerated by resting in divine supremacy.

Jesus said, "Come to me, all of you who are weary and carry heavy burdens, and I will give you rest."
—Matthew 11:28 NLT

God is always on duty. He never sleeps, so rest assured that you can sleep comfortably. He wants you to get a proper amount of sleep so that you can be at rest in your soul.

Dear friend, guard Clear Thinking and Common Sense with your life; don't for a minute lose sight of them. They'll keep your soul alive and well, they'll keep you fit and attractive. You'll travel safely, you'll neither tire nor trip. You'll take afternoon naps without a worry, you'll enjoy a good night's sleep.
—Proverbs 3:21-24

Prayer and Praise / Thankful Thoughts: _____

_____

_____

_____

We live in a day and age where we treat sleep as a luxury we can't afford, but studies indicate that sleep deprivation increases the risk of type 2 diabetes, high blood pressure, obesity, memory loss, stress, and premature aging. The truth is, sleep is as important to your body as diet and exercise.

So are you sleep-deprived? Do you suffer from exhaustion, fatigue, an inability to concentrate, or short-term memory loss? Do you make mistakes that should be avoidable? Do you become tongue-twisted and have difficulty speaking? If you answered "yes" to two or more questions, you are in need of more sleep. Try one or more of the following suggestions for a better night's rest:

- Relax by soaking in a hot lavender bath and using a lavender scent on your pillowcase.

- Go to bed earlier. This has little to no effect on your body's internal clock, unlike sleeping in late.

- Avoid snacking before bedtime. Snacking raises blood sugar, which inhibits sleep.

- Avoid caffeine and alcohol. Caffeine prevents sleep. Although alcohol may make you feel drowsy, it will wake you up hours later and prevent you from entering into deep sleep.

- Exercise at least 30 minutes a day. However, exercising too close to bedtime will keep you awake.

- Wear socks to bed. Feet have the poorest circulation of any body part. When they get cold, you wake up. As an added bonus, apply foot cream before you put on your socks. This will soften your feet as you sleep.

- If you read before you go to bed, make sure you avoid mystery or suspense novels that can keep you awake.

- Don't watch TV in your bedroom. Television stimulates the brain, which can prolong getting to sleep.

- Keep a journal next to the bed so you can empty your mind on paper before you go to sleep.

Be good to yourself and get a good night's rest. It's time to wake up to the fact that you *need* more sleep.

MakeOver Minute #18
UNDER THE CRUNCH

Is your faith a little flat? Do you experience bouts of disbelief or lack of trust? With the right exercises, you can work out your faith and steadily grow from flabby to fabulous!

- **Word crunch:** Study the Word of God on a consistent basis. "Study to show thyself approved unto God, a workman that needeth not to be ashamed, rightly dividing the word of truth" (2 Timothy 2:15 KJV).

- **Prayer crunch:** Pray—pray—pray! "Pray without ceasing" (1 Thessalonians 5:17 NKJV)

- **Decision crunch:** Choose to practice what you preach. "Are you willing to recognize, you foolish fellow, that faith without works is useless?" (James 2:20 NASB).

- **Reminded (in a) crunch:** Journal God's faithfulness to you. "Write them deep within your heart" (Proverbs 7:3 NLT).

- **Time crunch:** Make the time to share your faith with others. "I want you to give special emphasis to these matters, so that those who believe in God may be concerned with giving their time to doing good deeds, which are good and useful for everyone" (Titus 3:8 GNT).

Work your faith into what you say and do, and you'll remain faithfully fit.

Stay clear of silly stories that get dressed up as religion. Exercise daily in God—no spiritual flabbiness, please!

—1 Timothy 4:7

Prayer and Praise / Thankful Thoughts: _____

_____

_____

_____

Have you ever longed for a flat stomach, or least one that is not so flabby? The following abdominal exercises done in 12 to 16 repetitions will work the upper and lower ab muscles, giving you a well-toned tummy. You do not have to perform the exercises in the sequence in which they are given. You do, however, need to complete all of them in one 20-minute session four to five times a week in order for them to be effective.

1. **Normal crunches:** Lie down (looking up) and put your hands behind your neck, being careful not to pull on your neck. Bend your knees and keep your feet flat on the floor. Lift your shoulders to a 30-degree angle and hold for three seconds. Return to a resting position. Repeat.

2. **Leg-lift crunches:** Lie down (looking up) and stretch your arms over your head while holding on to something, such as the bottom edge of a sofa, that helps you to brace yourself as you slowly lift and lower your legs without touching the floor. Hold your legs perpendicular to the floor as long as you can between repetitions.

3. **Bridge crunches:** Lie down (looking up) with your knees bent and feet flat on the floor, hip-width apart. Squeeze your bottom as you push it up, lifting your hips toward the ceiling. Repeat.

4. **Plank crunch:** Lie face down, resting on your forearms with your hands clasped. Push up off the floor, resting on your forearms and toes. Keep your back flat and in a straight line from head to heels. (Don't stick your bottom in the air.) Hold for 30 to 60 seconds. Repeat twice.

5. **Rowing crunches:** Sit on the floor with your arms extended out in front of you. Bend your knees and raise your feet off the floor. Next, pull your arms and legs back and forth in a rowing motion while balancing on your bottom. Repeat 12 to 16 times.

6. **Vertical-leg crunches:** Lie down (looking up) and extend your legs straight up with your knees crossed. Put your hands behind your neck, being careful not to pull on your neck. Slowly lift your shoulder blades off the floor, raising your chest toward the ceiling while pushing your bellybutton towards your spine. Slowly relax and repeat.

7. **Marching crunches:** Lie down (looking up) with your hands next to your sides. Bring your left knee to your chest as you extend your right leg. Next, switch sides. Bring your right leg to your chest as you extend your left leg. (This should resemble a marching motion.) Repeat.

8. **Torso-twist crunch:** Sit on the floor with your knees bent and feet lifted slightly off the floor. Twist from side to side, touching the floor with your fingertips each time you rotate from left to right. Repeat.

Workouts are important to your overall well-being, but before you get started, consult a physician about what would work best for you.

MakeOver Minute #19
SHOW YOUR TRUE COLORS

God said…"When I see the rainbow in the clouds, I will remember the eternal covenant between God and every living creature on earth."

—Genesis 9:12-16 NLT

God put His true colors on display when He gave us the rainbow of promise. We read in Genesis chapter 6 that the world became so evil and corrupt that God became sorry He had ever created mankind. Noah, however, lived to love and obey Him.

What if God had come to *you* and said, "I need you to build an ark because it's going to rain." First of all, remember that up until this point in time, there was no such thing as rain. Secondly, what on earth was an ark? Yet we read that Noah never questioned a thing. He just got busy following God's directions. When your true colors are put to the test, how do you respond? So, the next time you see the beauty of the rainbow, be reminded that God's covenants are colored in truth and that He desires your faithfulness to Him.

I have placed my rainbow in the clouds. It is the sign of my permanent promise to you and to all the earth.

—Genesis 9:13 NLT

Prayer and Praise / Thankful Thoughts: _____

_____

_____

_____

Each one of us has our own set of true colors—colors that make us look our best even on days when we feel our worst. Wearing colors that enhance your natural skin tone flatters your face, enhancing your main point of communication.

Color seasons are divided into two categories—warm and cool. Members of the "warm" color family have natural gold undertones in their skin.

Members of the "cool" family have blue undertones. To determine whether you are "warm" or "cool," follow these simple instructions.

1. Remove all traces of makeup and pull your hair completely away from your face.

2. Drape yourself in a cream-colored piece of fabric. Hold it near your face and observe yourself in a mirror. Make the same observations using a bright white piece of fabric.

3. Now, ask yourself these questions. Which fabric makes your face appear redder and blotchier—beige or white? Which fabric makes your skin appear creamier and more even-toned? If you answered beige to question number one and bright white to question number two, you are a member of the "cool" family. If you answered bright white first and beige second, you are a member of the "warm" family.

If you are a member of the "warm" family, then your colors will be in either the "autumn" or "spring" category. Both of these color seasons consist of gold undertones but contain different color intensities. However, if you are a member of the "cool" family, then your colors will be in either the "winter" or "summer" color category. Both of these color seasons consist of blue undertones but contain different color intensities. To determine your season, hold an assortment of colors from either the "warm" autumn (rich and dark) and spring (light and bright), or "cool" winter (rich and dark) and summer (light and bright) up to your clean, makeup-free face. Now, select the season that looks best against your skin tone. If you cannot decide on your own, ask a friend's opinion.

- **Autumn** colors are made up of rich, dark shades of brown, rust, olive, orange, orange-red, and beige.

- **Spring** is defined by a lighter color value, which boasts the bright hues of brown, rust, olive, orange, orange-red, and tan.

- **Winter** colors are made up of rich and dark shades of charcoal gray, purple, navy blue, blue-red, black, and bright white.

- **Summer** colors consist of light gray, lavender, soft blue-gray, and a hint of pink, berry red, and bright white.

Remember, the goal is to wear the color instead of allowing the color to wear you.

MakeOver Minute #20
KEEPING TIME

There is a time for everything—especially for God. A number of years ago, I learned that when you put God first, everything else falls into place. This unexplainable phenomenon is best explained by a very simple children's object lesson.

Gather up one baby food jar, one walnut in its shell, some uncooked rice, and a bowl. Put the walnut into the empty baby food jar. This represents God being put first in your life. Next, add enough rice to fill the jar. The rice represents everything else that fills in your schedule. Notice that when you place the walnut—which represents God—into the jar first, the rice—which represents everything else in your life—easily fills in all around the walnut.

Now, empty the contents of the jar into the bowl. Next, put the rice into the jar first, then try to squeeze the walnut in. It won't work. It's the same in life. If we dedicate our time and energy to everything else first, we won't have time for God. Keep this jar in a prominent place in your home so it can be a reminder that you must always put God first in your life.

Each one of us has the same amount of time to manage, but how you schedule your time is totally up to you. Even in the midst of emergencies, you have the ability to readjust and carry on when you put your mind to it. Orchestrating your schedule takes planning, which is one of the most valuable tools a woman can learn in order to bring structure to her life. So, get busy and start planning today. Remember that when you put God first, you can relax knowing everything is under His control.

Instead, be concerned above everything else with the Kingdom of God and with what he requires of you, and he will provide you with all these other things.

—Matthew 6:33 GNT

There is a time for everything, a season for every activity under heaven.

—Ecclesiastes 3:1 NLT

_____

_____

_____

Are you on overload? Is your life off-balance and out-of-control busy? Do you meet yourself both coming and going? Well, you're not alone. Today's typical woman is busier now than ever before. Her life is pulled in numerous directions between work, home, kids, extracurricular activities, and church. There never seem to be enough hours in a day! If you consider that you need at least 8 hours of sleep in a 24-hour period, plus you work a job 8 hours, you've now accounted for 16 hours, which leaves you just 8 hours to accomplish everything else.

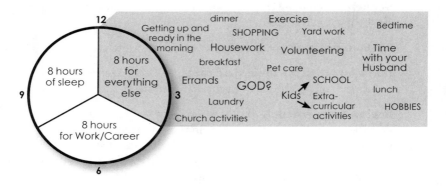

As you can see from the diagram, without applying some sort of structure to your day, your schedule will manage you instead of you managing your schedule. The first thing you need is a family calendar placed in a prominent area of your home, such as on the fridge. The second thing you need is a different color marker for each family member so you can differentiate between each person's activities. Now, it's time to fill in your calendar. As you do, here are some things to consider:

- **Reorganizing work.** If you work outside the home, consider whether or not your career interferes too much with family time. If it does, it may be time for a change in your work schedule. Organize your work schedule to help you manage better at home.

- **Prioritize.** Start with the most important items and work down from there. Your schedule should reflect your values.

- **Simplify your Sundays.** Make them a day of rest, the way God intended them to be.

- **Avoid procrastination as well as unnecessary stress.** Don't leave things till the last minute.

- **Divide up responsibilities between family members.** Even little ones can learn to pick up their toys.

- **Don't sweat the small stuff.** Remember what's important, and don't get carried away with things that don't matter.

- **Get help if you need it.** It's okay to hire a housekeeper or gardening service if you can afford it.

- **Set boundaries.** Remember, "no" is a complete sentence.

- **Don't forget to schedule time for *you***—time to reflect on God, and time to relax and recharge your own batteries.

- **Review your schedule.** Is there anything you can cut out? For example, do your kids want to take piano lessons, or do you want them to? For two years, I forced my son to take violin lessons. One day I finally gave up the battle, which was definitely the right thing to do. Our lives became more peaceful and less chaotic.

Balance brings beauty into your life. Find the right balance that works for you, and remember to celebrate your successes instead of dwelling on your shortcomings. Life is too short to be caught off-balance!

MakeOver Minute #21
TONE UP

Once you've accepted Jesus as your Savior and received pardon for your sins, a purification process has begun. With a skin-care routine, you wash your face to get rid of dirt, then apply toner to bring leftover impurities to the surface so they can be removed as well. This process never fails to give your skin a fresh, clean start.

A similar process happens as you mature in your Christian faith. Even after you invite Christ into your life, you still continue to sin. But the Holy Spirit acts as spiritual toner, cleaning up your life by penetrating the pores of your soul and bringing sin to the surface so you can turn from it.

I advise you to live according to your new life in the Holy Spirit. Then you won't be doing what your sinful nature craves.

—Galatians 5:16 NLT

God uses hardships to test us and bring our personal hangups to the surface so He can restore us and give us a fresh start. He also wants us to know that He will support, strengthen, and establish us through all life has to offer. Has the Holy Spirit brought anything to mind that you need to deal with? You don't need to sweat it any longer. Just give it to God, and be refreshed and renewed.

After you have suffered for a little while, the God of all grace, who has called you to his eternal glory in Christ, will himself restore, support, strengthen, and establish you.

—1 Peter 5:10 NRS

Prayer and Praise / Thankful Thoughts: _____

_____

_____

_____

Toner for your skin works like the rinse cycle on your washing machine. It penetrates your pores, refreshing and cooling your skin while clearing away excess oil, impurities, and dead skin cells missed by your cleanser. Toner also balances your skin's pH level (its acid level, which repels bacteria from the surface). When you wash your face, your skin's pH level becomes unbalanced. It can take an hour or more for the skin to repair itself, but toner instantly restores the pH level.

Toners are formulated for a variety of skin types—dry, normal, oily, and sensitive. You can either choose from a wide selection in the store, or you can formulate one of your own. No matter which type of toner you choose, use a cotton ball or pad to gently apply toner after washing your face and before moisturizing. Never use toner near the sensitive skin around your eyes.

Here are some of my favorite homemade toners containing pure, organic ingredients:

- **Rose toner** works wonders for dry-to-normal skin types. Mix together one-and-three-quarter cups witch hazel, one-quarter cup dried rose petals, and three sprigs of fresh rosemary. Allow to stand for ten minutes. Mix a second time, then strain. Apply to clean skin without rinsing.

- **Green-tea toner** is excellent for aging skin. Bring one-half cup of pure spring water to a boil. Place either two teaspoons of loose green tea leaves or one green tea bag in a cup, then pour the boiling water over the tea. Allow to steep for five minutes. Strain the tea, then let it cool to room temperature. Apply to clean skin without rinsing.

- **Honey-and-apple toner** brings help to combination or oily skin. In a blender, puree one small apple (peeled and cored) and two tablespoons of honey. Smooth this mixture over a clean face and leave on for 12 minutes. Rinse off with cool water.

Good, old-fashioned sweat has always been a natural way for your body to cleanse itself as perspiration releases dirt from your pores. That's why post-workout is always a good time to invigorate your skin with a refreshing toner.

MakeOver Minute #22
WATER WORKS

Water is the essence of both our physical and spiritual lives. John chapter 4 tells the story of the woman at the well—a social outcast who had been married five times and was living with man number six at the time she encountered Christ. It was around noon when she met Jesus at the well. Women in those times typically drew water at dawn and at dusk, but this woman most likely went out in the heat of the day to avoid the jeering of other women.

Jesus initiated the conversation by asking the woman for a drink. She was taken aback by the request. After all, she was a Samaritan, and it was a known fact that Jews had nothing to do with Samaritans. And neither did men fraternize with women. "How is it that You, being a Jew, ask a drink from me, a Samaritan woman?" the woman asked.

Jesus answered, "If you knew the gift of God, and who it is who says to you, 'Give Me a drink,' you would have asked Him, and He would have given you living water...the water that I shall give you will become in you a fountain of water springing up into everlasting life."

The woman had gone to the well to fetch a jug of water, but instead what she found was a cup of living water for her soul. Her sins were washed away by Jesus Himself. No matter who we are or what we have done, God is always merciful when we come to Him thirsty for forgiveness. When we drink from the cup of living water, we will say, "It is well with my soul."

Jesus answered, "If you knew the generosity of God and who I am, you would be asking me for a drink, and I would give you fresh, living water."
—John 4:10

Prayer and Praise / Thankful Thoughts: _____

_____

_____

_____

Water is essential to life. Without water, nothing can live. Next to oxygen, water is the most important element that sustains us. Water accounts for 60 percent of our bodies, which is two-thirds of our total body weight! When you drink water, it truly does become you. Proper hydration keeps the body running. And water has numerous benefits—it boosts our metabolism, reduces constipation, lowers the risk of colon, bladder, and breast cancer, decreases joint pain, and flushes toxins from our system. It even encourages weight loss and healthy skin. Water works!

With just a 2 percent drop in our body's optimal water requirements, we start to feel the effects of dehydration—headaches, stomachaches, loss of energy, fatigue, even short-term memory loss. You can live without food for approximately a month but without water for only a week. Water is our lifeblood. In fact, our blood's 83 percent water content enables us to digest our food, control our body temperature, and transport waste. The bottom line? Drink enough water!

Drinking water—specifically, eight 8-ounce glasses a day—has definite beauty benefits. Ask any supermodel how she maintains her weight and good skin and—while answers may vary to some extent—she's sure to be a water drinker. Water flushes impurities from your skin, giving it a clear, healthy radiance that makes your skin look younger. Dry, saggy skin plumps up when it's hydrated. Proper water intake also suppresses your appetite, which naturally helps the body metabolize stored fat. For every 25 pounds of excess weight you carry, you should drink an additional eight ounces of water per day.

And if you're tired of drinking water or just don't care for the taste? Give it a twist with a squeeze of lemon or lime!

MakeOver Minute #23
BOSOM BUDDIES

My fabulous friend Rose and I have a great story that illustrates our friendship. One day while we were out shopping—in the lingerie department, of all things—Rose picked up a pretty pink bra and said, "Tammy, you're like this bra." *"What?"* I asked. She grinned. "You *lift* my spirits, *support* me through the good times and the bad, help *shape* who I am, and even though we live on *separate* coasts we still remain the best of friends. We're bosom buddies!"

I want you to think of three things you look for in a friend. Then ask yourself, *Do I meet my own criteria for what I want in a friend?*

A true friend measures up. A true friend loves you through the ups and downs, the good and the bad, the highs and lows, and everything in between. A true friend fills your cup when you are running on empty and never asks for anything in return.

A friend is devoted, a friend is true,
A friend loves you no matter what you might do.
That friend is Jesus, He'll walk at your side
And lovingly listen as you confide.
He'll never leave you, He's there with you now,
He's promised to save you, this is His vow.

—Tammy Bennett

Some friends play at friendship but a true friend sticks
closer than one's nearest kin.

—Proverbs 18:24 NRS

Prayer and Praise / Thankful Thoughts: _____

_____

_____

_____

Did you know that eight out of ten women wear the wrong size bra? Chances are, the bra you have on right now isn't the right size for you! A properly fitting bra will comfortably lift, support, separate, and shape your figure in a flattering fashion.

Two measurements determine your correct bra size—the band measurement and the cup measurement. The band measurement is based on the size of your frame, and the cup measurement is calculated by measuring the fullest part of your breast.

To get started, you will need a seamstress's measuring tape and a pencil. First, keeping the tape measure smooth and taut, measure around your rib cage just beneath your bosom, being careful not to include any breast tissue in the measurement. Record your chest measurement in inches. If the measurement is an odd number, add five to it. If it's even, add six to it in order to find your band size. Band sizes run only in even numbers. That's why you must add either five or six to your chest measurement. For example if your chest size measures 29 inches, add five to get a 34-inch band size.

Next, measure all the way around your chest at the fullest part of your bustline. To get an accurate measurement, hold the tape measure straight but not so tight that it squashes your breasts together. Record your bustline measurement in inches. The difference between the bustline measurement and the chest measurement determines your cup size. To calculate, subtract your chest measurement from your bustline measurement. Each inch of difference is equal to one cup size:

less than 1 inch = AA cup	3 inches = C cup
1 inch = A cup	4 inches = D cup
2 inches = B cup	5 inches = DD cup

Even though this method of measurement is quite accurate, I still recommend you try on bras in at least three different sizes to get the perfect fit. For instance, if you measure a 34B, also try on a 36A and a 32C. The proper size for you will depend on the manufacturer's sizing and the style of bra you choose.

So how does your current bra measure up? Are you wearing the right size and style for your shape, or is it time to visit the lingerie department?

MakeOver Minute #24
BODY LANGUAGE

Body language is so important—especially within the church body! As a navy wife, I have moved many times. With those moves came lots of visiting churches. Church shopping is a grueling experience at best, but when a church body sends out positive vibes, it makes the process easier. Body language determines whether a church has a friendly, welcoming atmosphere or seems more like an uninviting institution.

> As God's chosen people, holy and dearly loved, clothe yourselves with compassion, kindness, humility, gentleness and patience. Bear with each other and forgive whatever grievances you may have against one another. Forgive as the Lord forgave you. And over all these virtues put on love, which binds them all together in perfect unity.
>
> —Colossians 3:12-14 NIV

Here, God tells us what He expects from His chosen—how we should conduct ourselves within the body of Christ so that we are an encouragement to each other and to outsiders as well. God wants our actions to back up our words and vice versa. We must be approachable in order to share the love of Christ, which means we need to practice positive body language at opportune times. When we do this, we bring praise and thanksgiving to God.

> Whatever you do, whether in word or deed, do it all in the name of the Lord Jesus, giving thanks to God the Father through Him.
>
> —Colossians 3:17 NIV

Prayer and Praise / Thankful Thoughts: _____

_____

_____

_____

Your face and body are constantly communicating with those around you. In fact, usually without even realizing it, you are always reacting to the body lingo of others. The majority of our communication is done through facial expressions and posture. It is possible to say one thing and mean another—the sound of your voice, the way you position yourself, and the look in your eyes can give you away.

What messages are you sending to others through your body language? Are you happy and confident, or negative and distant? Your body language speaks volumes about who you are and how you're really feeling:

Positive body language:

- direct eye contact that shows interest in what someone else is saying
- relaxed brow
- corners of lips relaxed and turned upward
- arms uncrossed in an open gesture that says "welcome"
- leaning forward when someone is talking, which shows interest
- hands posed in an upward steeple manner, which symbolizes confidence
- hands posed in a downward steeple, which indicates interest in what others are saying
- mirroring others' body language—a gesture of friendship

Negative body language:

- Limited or no eye contact, which shows you're lying, distracted, uninterested, or having your space infringed upon
- tense brow
- frowns, fake or nervous smiles, and lips pressed together
- crossed arms—a closed gesture that signals protectiveness or that others are not welcome
- rigid posture, a sign of anxiousness
- finger-tapping, which shows boredom, agitation, or anxiety
- wringing of hands, showing that you have something to say or are too nervous to speak up
- fidgety or bouncing legs, a sign of uneasiness

The next time you have something to say, make sure your body lingo backs you up. Most importantly, use it to discern the attitudes of those around you.

MakeOver Minute #25
FOUNDATIONAL TRUTH

The key to great-looking makeup is found in using the perfect base. The same principle holds true in the life of a Christian. The right foundation grounds you for life when it is established on the truth of the Scriptures.

> These words I speak to you are not incidental additions to your life, homeowner improvements to your standard of living. They are foundational words, words to build a life on. If you work these words into your life, you are like a smart carpenter who built his house on solid rock. Rain poured down, the river flooded, a tornado hit—but nothing moved that house. It was fixed to the rock. But if you just use my words in Bible studies and don't work them into your life, you are like a stupid carpenter who built his house on the sandy beach. When a storm rolled in and the waves came up, it collapsed like a house of cards.
>
> —Matthew 7:24-28

Even though the two houses appear the same on the outside, their bases set them apart. It is their type, texture, and tone that make them different even though they seem the same.

First, the construction starts with the *type* of man who built each house. A *wise* man and a *foolish* man are the builders in this story.

Next comes the *texture*—the foundation on which the house is built. The wise man built his house on the solid *rock*. The foolish man built his house upon the shifting *sand*.

Third, we look at the *tone* of the household after the storm had come and gone. The wise man's household, though shaken, *remained secure*. The foolish man's household *crumbled* under the pressure of the storm.

A mother often sets the stage for her home. The foundation she creates can be compared to that of the parable above. She's either wise and builds her house on the solid rock so her household remains secure through the storms of life. Or she foolishly ignores the absolute truth of the Scriptures and builds her house on shifting ideals, which lead to its ruin.

*Unless the L*ORD *builds the house,*
they labor in vain who build it.

—Psalm 127:1 NASB

How is *your* house constructed? Will your household testify of your faith? Remember, when you cement your house in the Word, your foundation will not crumble under pressure but instead will keep you rock-solid.

These words I speak to you are not incidental additions to your
life…They are foundational words to build a life on. If you work
these words into your life, you are like a smart carpenter who built
his house on a solid rock.

—Matthew 7:24 MSG

Prayer and Praise / Thankful Thoughts: _____

_____

_____

_____

Next to taking good care of your skin, applying the proper foundation is the most important way to create radiant skin. A good foundation also sets the stage for the rest of your cosmetics. When your foundation is right, your makeup will look good. If it's off, everything else will be off, too. The ideal type of foundation brings balance to your skin tone and texture and establishes the perfect backdrop to your makeup. The challenge is finding the right type for your face. Foundation is the one cosmetic you don't want to skimp on or purchase without trying on first.

The easiest way to find the perfect foundation is to go to your local cosmetic counter with a mirror in hand and start trying on samples. You'll need to look for three things when choosing a foundation for your skin—type, texture, and tone.

- **Type:** The first thing to do when choosing a foundation is to pick one formulated for your skin type. Is your skin dry, normal, oily, or a combination (such as oily in the T-zone but normal otherwise)?

- **Tone:** Foundation should always match your natural skin tone. Is your skin color light, medium, or dark? Choose two foundations that fall within your color range, then try them on. Use a makeup sponge or your fingers to blend the foundation into your skin, carefully noting if either of them blends well into your jawline and hairline. You also might want to step outside into natural daylight and use the handheld mirror to double-check how they blend. If a foundation you try does not match your skin tone perfectly, wipe it off and try another one.

- **Texture:** The texture of your skin will determine the intensity of coverage you need. Is your skin soft, smooth, rough, pitted, scarred, or acne-prone? Your skin texture may change with hormones or the weather, so you might want to have more than one foundation on hand.

To create a flawless finish, follow these beauty tips used by makeup artists everywhere:

1. Use a makeup sponge to blend your foundation, being careful not to leave a makeup line around your hairline or along your jaw. Also, be sure to blend the foundation between your face and your neck so you don't look like you are wearing a makeup mask.

2. Apply foundation as a perfectly matched concealer by using either the thick, pasty foundation that forms around the base of the cap or by dabbing foundation directly on the area you want to conceal. Allow it to dry for five minutes, then apply your foundation as usual, gently patting and blending around the concealed area.

3. Set your foundation by gently dusting your face with a light layer of loose powder. This will help eliminate breakthrough shine and creates the perfect finish for other powdered cosmetics, such as blush.

Foundation is the base of great-looking skin. When you use the right type of foundation, your skin tone and texture will look its best whether you apply other cosmetics or not.

A popular slogan is, "If it feels good, do it," but does that make it right? Should we operate off feeling or fact? (I've talked to many women who never thought they'd be affected by breast cancer, but the fact is that one in three women are diagnosed with this disease.) Fact or feeling, true or false, right or wrong—how can you know for sure?

I love the verse Acts 17:11: "They searched the Scriptures day after day to check up on Paul and Silas, to see if they were really teaching the truth" (NLT).

The Bereans developed their own Bible Self-Exam (BSE). They operated off the *facts* found in the *Word of truth,* so they would know for sure what was *right.*

Prayer and Praise / Thankful Thoughts: _____

_____

_____

_____

Breast self-exams (BSEs) are an effective way of detecting breast cancer early, when it's most likely to be cured. Not all breast cancer can be found this way, but research indicates that women who perform their own monthly checkups are more likely to discover tumors that are smaller and at an earlier stage than those who don't. Breast self-examinations take practice, because until you become familiar with the look and feel of your own breasts, it is difficult to notice anything but very obvious changes.

To get started, pick a time three to five days following your menstrual cycle. This is when your breasts are least likely to be swollen and tender. If you no longer have periods, pick a date on the calendar—such as the number of the date you were born—and perform the exam on that same date every month. If you are breastfeeding, do the exam when your breasts are empty. Next, follow the suggested procedure below:

- **Checkup #1—look:** Start by standing up straight, with your hands on your hips, and look at your breasts in a mirror. Note the size, shape, color, and texture of each breast. It is normal to have one breast larger than the other. Are your breasts evenly shaped without any visible distortions such as swelling, dimpling, puckering, or bulging of skin? Has either nipple become inverted, red, swollen, sore, or developed a rash? Next, gently squeeze each nipple between your pointer finger and thumb to check for any discharge. If you note any abnormalities, be sure to discuss them with your doctor.

- **Checkup #2—feel:** Lie down on a flat surface and extend your right arm over your head in order to spread the breast tissue out more evenly. Using your three middle fingers, start out by lightly making dime-sized circles around your nipple, working outward in a spiral rotation. Next, apply a deep pressure and do the breast check a second time. As you move your hand, be careful to keep your fingers firmly planted on your breast at all times so you don't miss a spot. Be careful to cover the entire breast area spot by spot. The area stretches from the armpit to the breastbone and the collarbone to the bra line. Repeat this same process on the other breast. Do not panic if you discover a lump or thickening. Many women have lumpy breasts. In fact, the majority of all breast lumps removed are benign. Nevertheless, do not take any chances—report any concerns you may have to your doctor at once.

- **Checkup #3—go:** Annual checkups with your health-care provider are also necessary! Between the ages of 20 and 40, women should have clinical breast exams performed by a health-care professional every three years, and then once a year from age 40 on. Mammograms are necessary every year starting at age 40, sooner if you are at risk due to a family history of breast cancer. Discuss your family history and any concerns with your health-care provider.

Breast self-exams—or BSEs—take only a few minutes, but they are extremely important. (For more information, visit www.komen.org.)

MakeOver Minute #27
VISUAL EFFECTS

I once purchased an item on E-Bay listed as a Swarovski crystal. Once I received it, though, I quickly discovered it was a fake. Even though the item looked identical to a genuine Swarovski, it was not authentic—it was a counterfeit.

Sometimes people are like that crystal. They learn to fake it—and fake it well. They manage to look good on the surface, but they are not authentic. And sometimes we go to church and Bible studies, trying to impersonate perfection. In fact, sometimes we're so good at faking it that we fool ourselves along with everyone else. But we never fool God.

You can fake it in fashion, but not in faith. It may be true that you can fool some of the people some of the time, but you can't fool God at all. Focus in on Him and who He wants you to be, and stop pretending. Get real. Be faithful to God, honest with others, and happier with yourself.

I, GOD, search the heart and examine the mind. I get to the heart of the human. I get to the root of things. I treat them as they really are, not as they pretend to be.

—Jeremiah 17:10

Prayer and Praise / Thankful Thoughts: _____

_____

_____

_____

It seems no matter what size we are, we are always striving to look thinner. Did you know that by simply putting on your wardrobe, you can take off weight? The following fashion tips will help you instantly shed ten pounds without going to the gym. And the improvement in your appearance will be even more real when you allow your true, honest, inside self to show through.

- Use self-tanner to visually slim down and contour the body.

- Stand up straight. Good posture literally adds inches to your height.

- Create a vertical line by wearing a monochromatic color that goes well with your skin tone. For example, wear the same color shirt, pants, shoes, or skirt with a jacket of a different color. This creates a vertical line that enhances your figure and makes you appear trimmer.

- Elongate your legs with high heels that are the same color as your pants or skirt. This makes your legs look longer and leaner. If heels are not your thing, shoes with pointed toes visually slim you down.

- Wear nylon-and-Lycra-blend support underwear. The tight weave smooths your torso, firms and lifts your bottom, shapes your waist, and hides those love handles. This type of underwear comes in all shapes and sizes to complement any wardrobe.

- Wear clothes that fit. Clothes that are too tight make you look like a bulgy sausage, and baggy clothing makes you appear dumpy and shapeless. If your hips are bigger than your waist, wear pants that fit your hips with a shirt that covers the ill-fitting waistband.

- Wear jeans that complement your bottom by choosing pockets that are proportionately the same size as your seat. For example, if you are trying to camouflage a larger area, steer clear of small pockets. Instead, choose jeans with bigger pockets situated lower on the seat to give your bottom an instant lift.

- Avoid wearing horizontal stripes, large and flashy prints, pleats, ruffles, and clingy fabrics.

- If you have a double chin, avoid crew necks, turtlenecks, and necklaces that highlight this area.

- If you have a large tummy, don't accessorize it with a wide, flashy belt.

The goal here is to fake away the pounds by dressing to accentuate the positive and disguise the negative. Although what you're seeing isn't necessarily real, it will make you look good and feel better about yourself.

MakeOver Minute #28
FIRST IMPRESSIONS

We are ambassadors for Christ.
—2 Corinthians 5:20 NASB

We communicate Christ in the way we live out our lives on a day-to-day basis. This is why first impressions are so important. Initial behavior either lends credibility to Christ and Christianity, or it totally disenchants those who are watching us.

Have you ever found yourself in a frustrating situation where you could 1) easily lose it or 2) take a deep breath and maintain your composure? It's a tough spot to be in, but the payoff can be rewarding when you choose to make a good impression and impersonate Christ.

Be imitators of God as dear children.
—Ephesians 5:1 NKJV

Whether you're aware of it or not, people are constantly watching you. They notice when you behave differently than what is normally expected. For example, I travel quite frequently, and air travel brings unexpected flight delays and cancellations and the inevitable rebooking of flights. It's often during the rebooking process that I encounter angry individuals taking out their frustrations on the rebooking agent. I was once in the midst of this process when the agent said to me, "Thank you for not being like everyone else. You've been so nice through this whole thing, and it was a pleasure to serve you." A few weeks later, as I was checking in at the airport, I encountered the same agent. She remembered me from the previous time. We started talking, and then and there I was able to share my faith because of the initial positive impression I had made on her.

We are ambassadors of Christ in all environments and in all situations, so it is important that we represent Him in all we say and do. Remember, you never get a second chance to make a first impression.

Prayer and Praise / Thankful Thoughts: _____

_____

_____

First impressions carry a lot of weight, and although they might not always be accurate, they happen anyway. So be prepared to make those first few seconds count in your favor.

You communicate who you are at a glance through a combination of characteristics. Here's how to connect with confidence in a way that intrigues instead of offends. Practice the following techniques so you are at ease with them, which will make others comfortable in your presence.

- **Always smile.** But don't overdo it! You'll be perceived as friendly and approachable if you look happy and content.

- **Practice good posture.** A poised presence conveys an air of self-assuredness, respectability, and calmness, which never fails to attract favorable attention.

- **Make sure you're well-groomed.** All aspects of personal neatness and hygiene are especially important to whether or not you make a good impression.

- **Confident introductions are key.** A firm handshake is a sign of self-confidence, and direct eye contact signifies respect for the person on the receiving end.

- **Put others first.** Learn to listen as much as you talk! Do not talk about yourself. Self-centered talk turns people off. Instead, show interest in other people, asking them questions about themselves.

- **Remain open.** Take care to not come across as close-minded. People take offense to a bigoted, intolerant attitude. Try to be nonjudgmental, and always keep any provoking opinions to yourself. Also, never present yourself as a know-it-all or someone who one-ups those involved in the conversation. Strive to listen to and affirm what others have to say instead of becoming a braggart.

You only get a few seconds to make a lasting impression, and although this may seem unfair—especially when you're having a bad day—it's just the way things are. There are no do-overs when it comes to first impressions, so be sure to get it right the first time!

YOU'VE GOT MAIL

I love to receive letters! My husband was in the navy before there were cell phones and e-mail, and letters were our only form of communication. It made my entire day when a letter from him arrived. I kept those letters close at hand, and whenever I was feeling especially lonely, I pulled them out and read them again and again. They were my sole source of comfort as I awaited his return.

Did you know that God wrote a love letter just to you? It is the Bible. His Word is a soul source of encouragement. It will uplift you when you are down. It will inspire you when you are looking for answers. It will enlighten you when you are facing a dilemma. And it will instruct you in the ways of God.

Every part of Scripture is God-breathed and useful one way or another—showing us truth, exposing our rebellion, correcting our mistakes, training us to live God's way.

—2 Timothy 3:16

The Bible is our personal love letter from God. We can read it again and again when we're feeling...

- **anxious** and **alone:** Psalm 27:10; Matthew 6:25-34; 28:20

- **angry** and **bitter:** Psalm 37:8-9; Proverbs 16:32; Ephesians 4:26

- **confused** and **uncertain:** Psalm 32:8; 138:8; Proverbs 3:5-6; Jeremiah 29:11; 2 Corinthians 4:8-10; Philippians 4:6-7; James 1:5

- **condemned:** John 8:10-11; 3:18; 5:24; Romans 8:1

- **down** and **depressed:** Isaiah 4:32; 61:3; 2 Corinthians 1:3-4

- **disappointed** and **dissatisfied:** Psalm 22:4-5; 130:1-5; Ephesians 3:20

- **feeble** and **weak:** 2 Corinthians 12:9

- **financially burdened:** Psalm 23:1; Philippians 4:19; 2 Corinthians 9:6-8

- **grieved** and **suffering loss:** Psalm 23:4; Matthew 5:4; 2 Thessalonians 2:16-17

- **happy** and **joyful:** Psalm 97:11; Nehemiah 8:10; John 15:10-11

- **hopeful:** Psalm 39:7; Hebrews 6:19; 1 Peter 1:3

- **impatient:** Psalm 40:1; Isaiah 40:31; Romans 15:4-5; Hebrews 10:35-37

- **inferior** and **insecure:** Ephesians 1:18-19; 3:18-19

- **lost** and **in need of direction:** Psalm 143:10; Proverbs 3:6; John 14:26

- **pained** and **suffering:** Romans 5:3-4; 1 Peter 2:20-21; 3:14

- **persecuted** and **wronged:** Psalm 103:6; Matthew 5:10; 1 Peter 4:12-13

- **remorseful** and **repentant:** 2 Chronicles 30:9; Isaiah 43:25; 1 John 1:9

- **shame** and **sorrow:** Psalm 34:5; 119:6

- **stress:** Psalm 142:3; James 1:2-4; 1 Peter 1:7

- **temptation:** Psalm 119:11; 1 Corinthians 10:12-13; Hebrews 4:14-16; 2 Peter 2:9

- **troubled** and **tested:** Psalm 34:17; 66:10; Isaiah 48:10; John 14:1,27

- a **wanting** and **longing:** Psalm 145:19; 119:37; 1 Peter 2:2

Like a cool drink of water when you're worn out and weary is a letter from a long-lost friend.

—Proverbs 25:25

_____

_____

_____

There was a time when letter writing was our primary source of communication, but times have changed and so have our forms of communication. Now, instead of a handwritten note, we send e-mails through cyberspace, sometimes to many recipients at a time. We also text message, using generic abbreviations and made-up words that are hard to understand if you're not up on the latest electronic lingo. Of course, we can always communicate by telephone—but even a phone call cannot compare to a sincerely expressed letter penned on a lovely piece of stationery.

Before my husband and I were engaged to be married, we wrote each other several letters a week even though we only lived an hour apart. I still have those letters, and I cherish every one of them. I've even shared some with our children, who laugh when they see how sappy their parents were even way back then.

I also keep letters, notes, and cards from family members and friends. Some of these dear people have since passed away, but they live on in their letters and bring a smile to my face, a tear to my eye, and fond memories that take me back to another time and place. That's the beauty of a letter. The paper may yellow with age, but the handwriting and the words leave behind a legacy that cannot be reproduced through other forms of communication. A letter is a gift forever.

When was the last time you wrote a good, old-fashioned letter to someone special?

Sincerely True

Do you have a friend you haven't talked to in a while,
Or a relative who could really use a smile?
What about a child who is just starting to read,
Or a teen who you could reach out to and lead?
Do you know someone who is elderly and alone,
Or a person who's somewhat depression-prone?
How about a neighbor from long ago,
Or a teacher who inspired you so—
And wouldn't your spouse welcome a love letter?
Do you know anyone you could make feel better?
When an e-mail or a phone call just won't do
Send a special note signed, "Sincerely True."

—Tammy Bennett

MakeOver Minute #30
PROVERBIAL SHOPPER

For years, we have looked to the multitalented Proverbs 31 woman for guidance. She was a dignified lady who loved God and brought honor to her husband. Scripture tells us that she successfully managed a household, cared for her servants, reached out to the poor, and exercised her entrepreneurial skills by making shrewd investments.

This lovely lady did it all, and she did it all *well*. Her husband trusted her, her children blessed her, her community valued her, and business people respected her. She did not waste time or money, and she considered her options and planned accordingly. She knew *what* her purpose was, and she sought to fulfill it. She knew *when* to get things done, and she did them. Most of all, she knew *where* her strength came from, and she never deviated from it.

What was her purpose? Her primary objective was to honor God, and she did this by managing her family and finances to the best of her ability. She didn't leave anything to chance but instead planned ahead and made prudent decisions that were productive for her household. Her good business sense allowed her the luxury of servants, the adornment of fine clothing, and the ability to contribute to the needy. Best of all, it earned her the trust of her husband and the respect of her family.

When did she have time? This woman kept a DayTimer, for sure! She wasted not a minute. She got up before dawn, and I imagine she accomplished more early in the morning than most people did in an entire day. She had a plan. Not only did she follow a daily schedule, but she also preplanned her family's future by making wise investments that would pay off in the long run. This lady didn't live for the here and now, but instead considered how her actions today would affect tomorrow.

Where did she get her motivation? The Proverbs 31 woman was motivated by her love for God. She displayed great character and strength in everything she said and did, which reflected who she was on the inside and spoke of her relationship with God. Her financial gain was driven by a wealth of spiritual understanding. She truly loved God—heart, soul, mind, and strength.

We have a lot to learn from this woman! Although she sets the standard high, it's not unattainable. She gives us something to reach for. With God, all things are possible. In Him and through Him, we can have all, be all, and do all that He has called us to.

> A good woman is hard to find, and worth far more than diamonds. Her husband trusts her without reserve, and never has reason to regret it. Never spiteful, she treats him generously all her life long. She shops around for the best yarns and cottons, and enjoys knitting and sewing. She's like a trading ship that sails to faraway places and brings back exotic surprises. She's up before dawn, preparing breakfast for her family and organizing her day. She looks over a field and buys it, then, with money she's put aside, plants a garden. First thing in the morning, she dresses for work, rolls up her sleeves, eager to get started. She senses the worth of her work, is in no hurry to call it quits for the day. She's skilled in the crafts of home and hearth, diligent in homemaking.
>
> She's quick to assist anyone in need, reaches out to help the poor. She doesn't worry about her family when it snows; their winter clothes are all mended and ready to wear. She makes her own clothing, and dresses in colorful linens and silks. Her husband is greatly respected when he deliberates with the city fathers. She designs gowns and sells them, brings the sweaters she knits to the dress shops.
>
> Her clothes are well-made and elegant, and she always faces tomorrow with a smile. When she speaks she has something worthwhile to say, and she always says it kindly. She keeps an eye on everyone in her household, and keeps them all busy and productive. Her children respect and bless her; her husband joins in with words of praise: "Many women have done wonderful things, but you've outclassed them all!"
>
> Charm can mislead and beauty soon fades. The woman
> to be admired and praised is the woman who lives
> in the Fear-of-God. Give her everything she deserves!
> Festoon her life with praises!
>
> —Proverbs 31:10-31

_____

_____

_____

Shopping can pay off if it's done right. In most cases, you don't need to pay full price for anything if you exercise a little shopping know-how. Between checking the newspaper ads, clipping coupons, comparing store brands, shopping discount retailers, and matching prices, you can save hundreds of dollars a year on the most basic of necessities.

Comparison shopping comes down to knowing *what, when,* and *where.* For example, let's say you need a new winter coat. The most inexpensive time to purchase a coat is after the first of the year, when winter clothing goes on clearance. But you can often do just as well if you shop certain discount stores or thrift shops. Once I purchased a $3750 mink fur—the original price tag was in the pocket—at a resale shop for only $25. Now, that's a real bargain!

- **What should you comparison shop for?** Everything! I've found that everything from food to health services differs in cost. When my kids needed braces, I couldn't believe the price differences I found for the same diagnosed service. I went to three different orthodontists, wise comparison shopping saved me $800.

- **What should you buy?** Buy only what you need. Don't buy something just because it's a great deal. About 20 years ago I bought a floor cloth stencil kit on a 90-percent-off sale. Know what? I still haven't used it! At the time I thought I might want to make a floor cloth someday, but "someday" hasn't come. To this day the kit remains unopened, collecting dust on a shelf in the garage.

- **When should you shop?** Depending on the item, sometimes you should shop when the item is in season, and sometimes you shouldn't. Take strawberries, for instance. When they're in season, your selection is plentiful and the price is at its lowest. But what if you're in the market for a snow blower? In that case, you should do a little advance planning and buy one at the end of the season. The selection may be limited, but the money saved is well worth the wait.

- **Where should you look?** This depends on the item you want. Out-of-the-ordinary places include yard sales, estate sales, auctions, roadside produce stands, E-Bay, or secondhand shops. The Internet can be beneficial not only for comparison shopping, but many stores offer special discounts that only apply to purchasing via their website.

Shopping is big business! And it works both ways. Shopping is not only profitable for the seller, but also lucrative for the buyer when she shops wisely. When you apply a little shopping sense, the cents you save will be yours to spend or to put away for a rainy day.

MakeOver Minute #31
FACE IT

Have you ever thought about how much time and effort we put into our faces? We often spend hours in front of the mirror, trying to improve how our faces look. We experiment with everything from facials to makeovers. Especially if we get a pimple, we go nuts trying to clear it up. The truth is, most of us spend a lot of time and money tending to our imperfections!

If you just listen and don't obey, it is like looking at your face in a mirror but doing nothing to improve your appearance. You see yourself, walk away, and forget what you look like.

—James 1:23-24 NLT

God leads us through His Word, prayer, and circumstances. Whether we seek His direction or not, He is still there leading 24/7. But are you listening? What is God calling you to? Does He want you to write a book, get involved in missions, lead a Bible study, reach out to a neighbor, volunteer in some capacity? Whatever it is, just *do* it! Don't miss the blessing that awaits you. Don't just walk away—instead, listen and obey!

If you do what it says and don't forget what you heard, then God will bless you for doing it.

—James 1:25 NLT

Prayer and Praise / Thankful Thoughts: _____

_____

_____

_____

There's nothing like going to the spa and being pampered with a professional facial. The expense, however, usually prevents us from enjoying this luxury very often. Facials can be costly, but you can get great-looking skin without the high price by doing your own facial in the convenience of your own home. Facials are easy to perform and on the average take only thirty minutes from start to finish. Basic facials consist of five steps—cleansing, exfoliating, steaming, masking, and moisturizing.

1. **Cleanse:** Thoroughly wash your face to remove any dirt and grime. Use a cleanser that is suitable for your skin type—dry, normal, oily, combination, or sensitive. (Cetaphil is good for all skin types.)

2. **Exfoliate:** Choose an exfoliant for your skin type. Using your fingertips, gently massage the exfoliating scrub over your face in a circular motion, being careful to avoid the delicate skin around your eyes. Rinse your face well, making sure you remove all traces of the gritty substance.

3. **Steam:** Wet a washcloth with very warm (but not hot) water, wring it out, lie back, and place it over your face. Leave it on for approximately two minutes, or until it has cooled off. This helps open up your pores.

4. **Mask:** Using your fingertips, gently apply a face mask suitable for your skin type. Do not apply it to the eye area. You can either purchase a ready-made mask at the store, or you can use one of the recipes below to make your own.

   - *For dry skin:* Mash together half an avocado and one-quarter cup of honey. Apply and leave on for ten minutes. Rinse off.

   - *For normal to combination skin:* Mix together two tablespoons rosewater, one tablespoon plain yogurt (not fat-free), and one tablespoon warm honey. Apply and leave on for ten minutes. Rinse well.

   - *For oily skin:* Blend together one teaspoon lemon juice, one egg white, one teaspoon honey, and half a cup of mashed strawberries. Apply and leave on for ten minutes. Rinse thoroughly.

   - *For sensitive skin:* Stir together one cup plain yogurt (not fat-free), and one-half cup basic oatmeal. Apply and leave on for fifteen minutes. Rinse off with warm water.

5. **Moisturize:** Smooth on a basic gentle moisturizer. Do not apply anything additional to your skin for at least two hours.

Typically, you should give yourself a home facial every other month. If you prefer going to the spa for a professional facial, you need one just four times a year—winter, spring, summer, and autumn.

MakeOver Minute #32
SUPPLEMENTAL BENEFITS

I studied Spanish for two years and even spent a summer in Mexico, where I was able to practice what I had been taught. Since then, I've barely used my Spanish at all. I've forgotten a great deal of it. The problem is, I have not supplemented my classroom learning with practical application.

This same principle can be applied to our faith. The book of 2 Peter gives us practical advice on putting our faith into daily practice. Like taking vitamins to round out a healthy diet, a healthy faith is supplemented with...

- **Virtue:** We are made righteous through Christ (2 Corinthians 5:21), yet attempting to live a virtuous life can only be accomplished when we choose to follow the Holy Spirit's prompting.

- **Knowledge:** Read and study the truth found in the Bible, then put it into practice (see James 4:17).

- **Self-control:** You can't always control what happens to you, but you *can* control the way you react to it (see Proverbs 16:32).

- **Steadfastness:** Perseverance on your own is difficult at best, but when you know that God is ultimately in control, staying the course becomes easier (see 1 Corinthians 15:58).

- **Godliness:** God is in us and with us, and we should continually be aware of His presence in our lives (see Proverbs 21:21).

- **Brotherly kindness:** The Bible directs us to love God and to love people. According to God's Word, you can't do one without the other (see 1 John 4:20).

- **Love:** God is love, and we love because we are of God. God does not call us to like others—the things they do and the things they say—but He *does* call us to love them unconditionally (see 1 John 4:7-8).

Get the optimum benefit out of your faith by putting all you know about it into practice. Be found faithful in your faith!

_____

_____

_____

Have you ever wondered if you are getting the proper nutrients your body needs to let it function efficiently and effectively? Recommended daily amounts of vitamins and minerals can be found in a balanced diet, but even then, it's hard to determine how many nutrients you're taking in from the foods you eat. Besides, some methods of cooking actually decrease the vitamin and mineral content of your food. This is where vitamin supplements come in. Taking a one-a-day multivitamin can help your body perform at its optimum level. Here are just a few of the associated benefits:

- Vitamin B complex, vitamin E, and vitamin C help support your adrenal glands, which helps you to combat stress.

- Calcium supplements and extra vitamin D lessen the risk of osteoporosis.

- If you do not spend at least 15 minutes a day outdoors, or if you live in a region with limited sunlight, consider taking a vitamin D supplement.

- Do you easily catch colds? Your immune system could probably use a boost of vitamin C.

- Hormonal problems are sometimes caused by a lack of vitamin B_6. Consult your doctor to find out if this is the case with you.

- If you suffer from anemia, you may need to take an iron supplement.

- Take calcium and magnesium to help eliminate leg cramps.

- The B vitamins can help fight heart disease and reduce the risk of certain types of cancer.

Before you start taking any type of supplement, consult your health-care provider. And always follow the directions on the label unless otherwise directed by your physician.

Makeover Minute #33
QUICK FIX

Have you ever noticed how an encouraging word works as a quick fix to almost any problem? Now, the problem won't automatically resolve itself—but kind words definitely do help!

The other day, I was having one of those "Murphy's Law" type of days—where anything that could go wrong, did go wrong. I was near my wit's end and just about ready to pull my hair out when one of my best girlfriends called me and helped me put my day in perspective. (Isn't it amazing how God can send us a phone call at just the right time?) She reminded me who is ultimately in control, and encouraged me that, although I had experienced some setbacks, I'd ultimately get through this—and ultimately be better off for the experience.

Proverbs 16:24 states, "Kind words are like honey—they cheer you up and make you feel strong" (CEV). Kind words are easy to swallow. Do you know anyone who could use a quick sweet-word fix? How about your husband—could he use a word of appreciation? Would your child like to hear the words, "Well done"? Perhaps your mother would just like to hear the sound of your voice. Maybe your boss could use a word of thanks, or a friend a word of advice. And your neighbor might just need a bit of friendly conversation.

Gracious speech is like clover honey—good taste to the soul, quick energy for the body.

—Proverbs 16:24

Prayer and Praise / Thankful Thoughts: _____

_____

_____

_____

Have you ever found yourself in a fashion pickle? You're just about to walk out the door when all of a sudden you chip a nail, dribble coffee on your blouse, or snag your sweater? All of us sometimes experience these little inconveniences, and although they're certainly annoying, with a little know-how you can take care of the problem. Below are some quick fixes to the most common beauty mishaps.

- When you need to hide a **zit,** use a concealer brush and cover the blemish with or opaque concealer. The brush allows you to target the blemish by gently tapping the tip directly onto and around the affected area. Next, dust oil-free powder over the spot to minimize shine and set the concealer.

- A **loose button** that's not too far gone can be secured with either a drop of nail glue or clear fingernail polish. Take care not to get it on the garment.

- A **spot on your outfit** can easily be cleaned off with a baby wipe or a Tide Pen.

- If you get a **snag in your clothing,** use a button threader to reach through and pull the snag to the underside of the garment.

- Another **chipped fingernail?** Quickly touch it up with matching polish, then zap it with a blow dryer.

- If you **break an artificial nail,** either glue it back on or disguise it with a Band-Aid.

- Have you ever put something on only to discover **an unraveling hem,** or maybe you've caught the hem on your heel and pulled it out yourself? In this case, heavy-duty, double-sided tape makes a great quick fix.

- Is a **sticky zipper** giving you fits? Rub it with a bar of soap or a pencil lead.

- **Pantyhose problems?** Avoid snags or runs by first smoothing your legs with lotion, then putting your hose on with gloves so you don't run a fingernail through them.

- Do you tend to get **makeup on your clothes** when getting dressed? Drape your head with a silk scarf, then pull your top over your head. This keeps your makeup on your face, plus it prevents your hair from getting messed up in the process.

- If you wake up to **puffy eyes,** use a dab of Preparation H to remedy the problem.

- Get rid of **stains on suede** by lightly rubbing a plain emery board in a back-and-forth motion until the stain is removed.

MakeOver Minute #34
IDENTITY CRISIS

Once you accept Jesus into your life, you have a new identity. You are a Christian—you have been invaded by the Holy Spirit. You are no longer on your own. You have the God of the universe living in you 24/7.

When you heard the true teaching—the Good News about your salvation—you believed in Christ. And in Christ, God put his special mark of ownership on you by giving you the Holy Spirit that he had promised.

—Ephesians 1:13 NCV

You have been given a new lease on life. Your old way of thinking is steadily being transformed by your faith in God. You now have someone You can totally put your trust in and fully rely on, day in, day out.

Now, are you identified by others as being in Christ? In other words, if someone—a neighbor, a co-worker, a classmate—described you, would they identify you as a Christian?

You have been set apart for God. You have been made right with God because of what the Lord Jesus Christ and the Spirit of our God have done for you.

—1 Corinthians 6:11 NLT

So dare to be set apart for God. Dare to be who God called you to be in Him and through Him. Dare to be different!

Christ's life showed me how, and enabled me to do it. I identified myself completely with him. Indeed, I have been crucified with Christ. Christ lives in me. The life you see me living is not "mine," but it is lived by faith in the Son of God, who loved me and gave himself for me.

—Galatians 2:20

_____

_____

_____

Dare to be different. How many times have you heard that one? It sounds good in theory, but when it comes to being yourself it gets a little scary. *What will people think?* we wonder. *What if they don't like me or think I'm weird? Suppose I look goofy?* We become so afraid of rejection that we'd rather morph into the uncomfortable than become comfortable with who we really are.

Have you ever been prompted to buy something you didn't really like or pass on something you wanted because you felt intimidated?

Sound crazy? Not really. All of us seek acceptance from others, and sometimes we do—or don't do—the darnedest things to get it. Just the other day I was out shopping and came across light-up flip-flops in adult sizes. You know the kind the kids wear, with soles that light up as you walk? I was thrilled! I'd always wished they made these in larger sizes. As I stood there trying to decide between pink and purple, a gal came up to me and said, "Aren't those the most ridiculous things you've ever seen?" I just kind of stood there, nodded, and said, "Yeah, they're pretty bizarre alright." I slowly walked away, thinking, *Maybe she's right—maybe they are too much for someone my age.* I mulled it over as I shopped, then finally decided, *I really do like those flip-flops, no matter how funky they are. Why should I allow a perfect stranger to influence my taste in shoes?* After all, not everyone likes the same things. So why not go with what appeals to me?

Peer pressure is real at all ages. Many of us are motivated by what others might think, and as a result our own individuality becomes extinct. Don't let this happen to you. Protect your identity by allowing your likes and dislikes to remain *yours.* Dare to be different—dare to be *you!*

MakeOver Minute #35
LIPSTICK TIPS

Did you know that your lipstick is a fun way to figure out your temperament? The most important thing about your lips is what they say—that's how most people judge you. Your words not only speak volumes about your personality, but they also identify your character as well. What do your lips say about you?

How you talk defines your God-given personality. The sanguine personality is a big talker and tends to exaggerate. The choleric personality can be bossy and opinionated. The melancholy personality is inclined to be critical and analytical. And the phlegmatic personality prefers to say nothing at all unless prompted to do so.

Before I formed you in the womb I knew you.

— Jeremiah 1:5 NKJV

What you say and how you say it forms your character. Are you truthful, or do you lie? Do you gossip, or can you keep a confidence? Do you belittle and come across judgmental, or do you encourage? Are you overbearing or soft-spoken? The answers to these questions give insight into whether or not you are a person of integrity. Unlike the personality you are born with, character is something you continue to develop throughout your life.

A gadabout gossip can't be trusted with a secret, but someone of integrity won't violate a confidence.

—Proverbs 11:13

Better is the poor who walks in his integrity than one who is perverse in his lips, and is a fool.

—Proverbs 19:1 NKJV

Your words and how you say them tip people off and give them insight into who you really are. What do your lips reveal about your personality? Do your words bring you honor, or do they discredit your character?

Set a guard, O Lord, over my mouth; keep watch
over the door of my lips.

—Psalm 141:3 NKJV

Prayer and Praise / Thankful Thoughts: _____

_____

_____

_____

A few years ago, I learned that you can tell a lot about a person by the shape of her lipstick tip. After further investigation into the personality types, I came up with my own list. Let's have a little fun! Pull out your tube of lipstick and compare the shape of its tip to those described below. What does your lipstick have to say about you?

- A **sanguine's** lipstick tip has a sharp-angled curve. She's outgoing and upbeat, quite creative, loves to talk, and is a great storyteller. She has a need to be the center of attention, falls in love easily, and isn't good at keeping time or sticking to a schedule.

- A sharp, angled tip can be found on a **choleric's** lipstick tube. She's highly opinionated and argumentative, displays high energy, and thrives on change. She's naturally an extrovert, a natural-born leader, and is a self-sufficient self-starter.

- A slanted tip that closely resembles the original shape of the lipstick defines a **melancholy's** tube. She's deep, thoughtful, and purposeful, with a tendency to fantasize. Preferring not to draw attention to herself, she is quiet, conscientious, operates best off a schedule, and follows the rules.

- A **phlegmatic's** lipstick tends to have a rounded, smooth tip. She's easygoing and easy to get along with, a good listener, and a peacemaker. She tends to be calm, cool, and collected, likes consistency, and is very likable.

MakeOver Minute #36
SUIT YOURSELF

My husband served in the United States Navy for 20-plus years, which means we moved our fair share of times. Although I enjoyed living in new places, one thing I didn't care for was shopping for a new church home. It wasn't until we understood the purpose of the church body that we were able to establish a list of requirements that narrowed down our choices. The purposes listed below showed us what to look for so we could avoid getting caught up in "entertain me" theology, as described in 2 Timothy 4:3-4. It helped us focus on making God our number-one priority.

- **Worshipping:** The first thing we are called to do as Christians is to love God with all our heart, soul, mind, and strength. However, the Bible says we should not be "avoiding worshipping together" (Hebrews 10:25), and the church is just the place to do it.

- **Learning:** Church is also a learning center: "Even if it was written in Scripture long ago, you can be sure it's written for *us*. God wants the combination of his steady, constant calling and warm, personal counsel in Scripture to come to characterize *us*" (Romans 15:4).

- **Growing:** A church should inspire spiritual maturity among believers by meeting them where they're at and helping them to grow from that point on: "You must crave pure spiritual milk so that you can grow into the fullness of your salvation" (1 Peter 2:2 NLT).

- **Serving:** The church should be a place that helps you discern your gifts, then equips you to use them in service to God: "Serve the Lord enthusiastically" (Romans 12:11 NLT).

- **Encouraging:** The church body should be one of your greatest sources of encouragement. It must offer prayer support and godly nurturing: "The one who proclaims God's message speaks to people and gives them help, encouragement, and comfort" (1 Corinthians 14:3 GNT).

So find a church that suits you—one that will inspire you to worship, learn, and grow—and it will be a great source of encouragement that helps you to fulfill the mission God has placed before you.

_____

_____

_____

When it comes to shopping for clothes, I've always enjoyed the mission. Swimsuit shopping, however, is a totally different story. I can remember hours spent in the dressing room trying on suit after suit, with each one looking worse than the last. It seemed like a never-ending process that usually ended in utter and complete failure. It wasn't until I understood the needs of my own body shape that I became successful at shopping for a swimsuit. Take my tips for finding a suit that flattens your tummy, fixes your flaws, and flatters your figure.

- Do you need a **tummy tuck?** Find a one-piece swimsuit with a supportive liner—such as spandex or Lycra—and a higher back to smooth and flatten your midsection. In addition, you may try a suit with jeweled details that draw your eye up and away from the area you wish to camouflage.

- Do you need **more up top?** Pair a padded print-tankini top with a solid-colored bottom. Your bust will look bigger and your bottom will appear smaller.

- Do you want to **create curves?** A v-neck wraparound suit gives the illusion of a curvy figure.

- Do you want to **appear taller?** Try on a solid-colored one-piece suit with a high-cut leg. This look will elongate your legs and torso.

- Do you want to **minimize your bottom?** Try a printed one-piece suit with a built-in or matching slimming skirt (avoid ruffles). Special note: The size of the print should match the size of your shape.

- Do you need **added support**? Choose a suit with wide straps and a built-in support bra.

Never dread swimwear shopping again! Instead, enter the dressing room with confidence, knowing you have the know-how to successfully accomplish your mission.

MakeOver Minute #37
HAIR BE GONE

When I think of hair removal, I'm reminded of the story of Samson and Delilah—Samson the superman and Delilah the seductress. Judges 13–16 tells all about Samson—his accomplishments as well as his failures. We see how, from his youth, he experienced victory after victory over the Philistines. We also note his weakness for women, which eventually led to his demise.

The Philistines grew tired of Samson's attacks and decided to go after him where he was most vulnerable. They hired Delilah to seduce him and discover his breaking point, which she successfully did. Delilah used her sexuality to manipulate and nag Samson into telling her the source of his physical strength.

> *"My hair has never been cut," he confessed, "for I was dedicated to God as a Nazarite from birth. If my head were shaved, my strength would leave me."...Delilah lulled Samson to sleep with his head in her lap, and she called in a man to shave off his hair, making his capture certain. And his strength left him.*
>
> —Judges 16:17,19 NLT

Samson was seized, his eyes were gouged out, and he was put on display at a Philistine pagan festival. When he pleaded with God to give him back his strength so he could destroy the temple—and all those in it—God heard his prayer. Samson pressed against the pillars with all his might, the temple came crashing down, and everyone in it perished—including Samson.

Can you identify with Samson or Delilah? Like Samson, are you consumed with pride? Or are you more like Delilah, consumed with selfishness and scheming to get your own way? No matter what, God is ready to hear your prayer and restore you to a right relationship with Him.

Prayer and Praise / Thankful Thoughts: _____
_____
_____
_____

Although many of us would like to remove unwanted hair permanently, the expense can be prohibitive. Instead, we resort to alternative methods for getting rid of unsightly hair. Try one or more of the following to see which method works best for you.

- **Bleaching**, although it does not remove the hair, does make the hair less noticeable. This is particularly effective on areas such as the upper lip, arms, and neck. Bleaching is performed by applying a specially formulated chemical peroxide to the desired area, which removes the pigment from the hair. This process can either be done professionally or at home with a kit purchased from your local beauty supply store.

- **Shaving** is the most popular but temporary hair-removal method. Its effect only lasts a few days before you start to feel blunt stubble again. When you shave, use an inexpensive hair conditioner as an alternative to shaving gel or soap. It will allow the razor to glide easily over the surface and leave your skin feeling silky and smooth.

- **Tweezing** can be time-consuming, but the hair takes longer to grow back in. Sometimes, if you pluck out hairs often enough, you may damage the hair follicle to the point where it stops producing hair altogether. Tweezers are commonly used on the eyebrow area, chin, and breasts. To minimize tweezing discomfort, pluck the hair immediately following a shower, while your pores are still open.

- **Depilatories** contain ingredients that break down the strength and structure of the hair bonds, literally melting it away so it can be easily wiped off. In addition to dissolving the hair, depilatories also remove dead cells from the surface of the skin. Popular brands such as Nair can be found at your local drugstore.

- **Waxing** is a more costly method of removing large amounts of hair for a period of about four weeks. I recommend having it done professionally, but you can also purchase kits for waxing at home. Warm wax is spread over the skin in the direction of the hair growth. The hair becomes embedded in the wax as it cools and then is quickly pulled off in the opposite direction of the hair growth.

MakeOver Minute #38
AGING GRACEFULLY

There is a fine line between aging and retiring. Many people believe the two go hand in hand, but while to a certain extent this is true, it definitely isn't the case with spiritual maturity. According to the Scriptures, we have a responsibility to minister to future generations until our time on earth is done.

Guide older women into lives of reverence so they end up as neither gossips nor drunks, but models of goodness. By looking at them, the younger women will know how to love their husbands and children, be virtuous and pure, keep a good house, be good wives. We don't want anyone looking down on God's Message because of their behavior.

—Titus 2:3-5

Years ago when I was twenty something, a dear friend and mentor said, "You are always older than someone who could benefit from your experience and know-how." That struck me as funny, because at the time I thought I had so much to learn before I could be of any value to anyone else. God, however, showed me otherwise. Right after that, the Lord brought a young teenage mom into my life who needed guidance I was able to offer.

The time to be effective is *now*. Be an encouragement to those who are younger, motivating them to live in a way that honors God. On the other hand, if you're the one who needs advice, seek out a godly mentor to guide you. Aging in spiritual grace helps you smooth out the wrinkles that life furrows your brow with. And—unlike age—spiritual maturity is something earned, not granted.

Prayer and Praise / Thankful Thoughts: _____

_____

_____

_____

The secret to youthful-looking skin is collagen, which has been called the skin's structural fiber. As we get older, that fiber breaks down and creates lines on the skin's surface. What causes this breakdown? Collagen's number-one enemy is the sun. In fact, dermatologists say that over 85 percent of wrinkles and age spots are a result of sun exposure. That's why they repeatedly encourage us to wear hats and use sunblock with an SPF of 15 or higher.

So what can you do if the damage has already been done? To discover the best renewal options, read on.

- **Vitamin A or retin-A** is your best defense against wrinkles and age spots. It's been proven to work better than any other skin-care product, but it is only available by prescription.

- **Retinol-A** is an over-the-counter product that contains nonprescription versions of vitamin A derivatives. Although not nearly as strong as retin-A, it can still help. Retinol-A can be found in various cosmetics as well as topical creams and lotions.

- **Alpha hydroxy and beta hydroxy acids (AHAs and BHAs)** facilitate the shedding of dead skin cells and can even trigger the production of collagen. The main difference between the two is their solubility. Alpha hydroxy is water soluble, and beta hydroxy is oil soluble. Alpha hydroxy acids work best on normal, sun-damaged skin that is not prone to breakouts. Beta hydroxy acids penetrate the pores to remove dead cells beneath the skin's surface and effectively fight blackheads and whiteheads. Like retinol-A, AHAs and BHAs can be found in a variety of over-the-counter products—from moisturizers to eye creams to foundation.

- **Vitamin K** is advertised to diminish the appearance of spider veins, skin discolorations, bruising, and scarring due to burns. It is also used to control blood clotting.

Maturity is the ability to think, speak and act your feelings within the bounds of dignity. The measure of your maturity is [not how many wrinkles you have but] how spiritual you become during the midst of your frustrations.
—Samuel Ullman (1840-1924)

MakeOver Minute #39
PEEL AND REVEAL

What lies beneath the surface of your intentions? If others could peel away your exterior, what would they find in your heart? Proverbs 31:30 declares, "A woman who fears the LORD, she shall be praised" (NKJV). To fear means to love, to love means to respect, and to respect means to obey. If you could apply a chemical peel to your intentions, would it reveal a love for God or a love for self? Try this three-step process:

1. **Cleanse:** Pray and ask God to forgive you for your pride and selfishness.

2. **Refine:** Refine your life by revealing your new mode of operation—backing your words with your actions. Others find it refreshing when you say what you mean and mean what you say.

3. **Protect:** Now it's time to protect what you've put into practice. Embrace God's love by loving Him to the best of your ability so that you can avoid the influence of the enemy.

When the Lord comes, he will bring our deepest secrets to light and will reveal our private motives. And then God will give to everyone whatever praise is due.

—1 Corinthians 4:5 NLT

Prayer and Praise / Thankful Thoughts: _____

_____

_____

_____

Chemical skin peels are used to treat topical skin conditions such as fine lines, wrinkles, age spots, acne, scars, sun-damaged skin, and discoloration. They work by removing the flawed outer layer of dead cells so that the fresh new skin beneath the surface is revealed, revitalizing your skin's appearance.

A variety of chemical peels are available, ranging from mild at-home treatments to more intense treatments performed by doctors and dermatologists. To determine the type of treatment you need, I recommend you consult your physician. If cost is of concern, you might give an at-home peel a try.

Affordable over-the-counter chemical peels are in high demand. Consequently, many manufacturers have formulated peels consisting of weaker concentrations of those ingredients found in physician-administered peels, so that you can receive like benefits at a lower cost in the comfort of your own home. Typical at-home chemical peel kits use a three-step process:

1. **Cleanse:** Step one includes using some type of cleansing or exfoliating scrub to gently remove dead cells, oil, and dirt from your skin's surface to purify and prepare it for the application of the chemical peel.

2. **Refine:** Next, you apply the chemical enzyme peel, which removes any remaining dead cells and leaves your skin's surface refined and refreshed.

3. **Protect:** The final step should always include applying an SPF 15 moisturizer, which will protect the radiant new skin from the environment and the harmful effects of the sun. Some kits include moisturizer, but even if you have to buy it at an additional charge, be sure not to skip this step.

As you work through the above three steps, keep in mind these precautions:

- Avoid the delicate skin around your eye area, lips, and nostrils.
- Do not use any type of chemical peel on damaged or irritated skin.
- If you develop a rash or irritation occurs during or after the peel, discontinue use and, if needed, consult a physician.
- Follow the manufacturer's directions concerning the application and use of the product.
- Keep the compounds out of the reach of children.

MakeOver Minute #40
CAN YOU HEAR ME NOW?

Although the science of mobile technology continues to advance, mobile communication has been around since the beginning of the world. In fact, scientific know-how will need to develop quite a bit before it becomes what we already have with God—total access 24/7, anywhere, with no interruptions or roaming fees.

I grew up with a party-line telephone system, which in our case meant five families sharing the same phone line, and in case of an emergency, there was no such thing as 9-1-1. Over the course of the last 25 years, telephone technology has changed tremendously. We've gone from party lines to individuals having their own cellular phone on which they can call, e-mail, and send text messages and photos.

This still doesn't compare to what we have with God—free total access all the time, with or without verbal communication. I can talk to God in the car, on the plane, in an elevator—even when I'm lounging in the pool!

Keep on praying.
—1 Thessalonians 5:17 NLT

Mobile communication is the answer to all your needs. You can call on God anytime, knowing you'll always get through, you'll never be cut off, and you'll always be heard. You never have to ask, "Can you hear me now?"

We can always talk to God with a thankful attitude, knowing that He will sustain us through everything throughout all of life. God's mobile service will never be terminated and will never, ever fail you.

Devote yourselves to prayer with an
alert mind and a thankful heart.

—Colossians 4:2 NLT

Prayer and Praise / Thankful Thoughts: _____

_____

_____

_____

Communicating on the run has become a way of life. Mobile or cellular phones have revolutionized our world, enabling us to stay connected with home, work, family, and friends from virtually anywhere and at any time. Personally, I depend on mine to catch up on telephone messages while I'm waiting in the car or at the airport. In fact, I've often wondered how I ever managed without one! Cell phones are indeed the latest and greatest accessory—one that promises not to go out of style anytime soon. And although they are available in a variety of sizes and colors, you can inexpensively personalize your phone with a little creativity. Accentuate it with everything from charms dangling from the antenna to beads you glue on yourself. I've decorated my plain little black model with pink and white sparkly beads, which totally accents my *pink* personality.

To decorate your phone with beads, you'll need beads (either a single color or a combination of colors to create your own pattern), nail glue (the kind used for artificial nails), a toothpick, and Sticky Tac (the type used to hang posters on the wall).

1. Affix a tiny, BB-size ball of Sticky Tac to the tip of the toothpick. This enables you to easily pick up and apply beads to your phone without getting glue on your fingers or on the top sides of the beads, which would reduce their shine and luster.

2. Use the Sticky Tac end of the toothpick to pick up a bead on its top side. Carefully apply a tiny dot of glue to the underside of the bead. Now, gently place the bead on the outside of the phone, constructing your design from the inside out and taking care not to cover the display buttons or the microphone.

3. Repeat the above step until the desired amount of beads have been applied. Then, allow the glue to dry for at least two hours before using your phone.

One important reminder before you proceed—if you alter your mobile phone in any way, the telephone company will not repair it, even if it is still under warranty.

Makeover Minute #41
BEIJING DIET

Our diets impact our lives. How we eat and what we eat affects our weight, our health, and our mode of operation. It's a simple fact—when you take in too much junk food, you feel junky, but when you eat right, you feel better.

As recorded in chapter 1 of the book of Daniel, Daniel made up his mind to adhere to his God-given diet and not defile his body with the rich food and strong drink offered by King Nebuchadnezzar. As a result, Daniel stood out and ended up having a profound impact upon history. His exemplary approach to life teaches two basic truths—know God's will, then do it.

Daniel made up his mind not to defile himself by eating the food and wine given to them by the king. He asked the chief official for permission to eat other things instead.
—Daniel 1:8 NLT

Daniel knew God personally and studied His ways so that he could implement them in his own life.

And God will have a profound impact on your life too when you commit to living a disciplined life for Him.

Prayer and Praise / Thankful Thoughts: _____

_____

_____

_____

A few years ago, I traveled to Beijing, China, and while I was there I noticed that the Chinese people do not have weight issues. The vast majority of the population is trim and fit without being weight-conscious. While in Beijing, I discovered what I believe to be the secret to healthy eating. The "Beijing diet," as I call it, consists of two simple techniques that require only a knife, chopsticks, and a little practice.

For the most part, the Chinese use sharp knives to cut their food into small, bite-sized pieces that are easy to pick up and eat with chopsticks. Chopsticks are the key to the Beijing diet—eating small, bite-size pieces with chopsticks slows down your pace so your brain can signal to your stomach that you're full. A typical Chinese meal consists of meats and vegetables as well as soup, rice, or noodles. You can either apply these techniques to your own main-course menus—minus the dessert, of course—or you can try the recipe below.

Sesame Chicken and Broccoli

1/4 cup soy sauce

2 tablespoons dry sherry (optional)

2 tablespoons sesame oil

1 clove garlic, minced

2 teaspoons fresh ginger root, minced

1 tablespoon sugar

1/4 cup sesame seeds, toasted

2 boneless, skinless chicken breasts, cut into bite-sized pieces

3 tablespoons peanut oil

1 cup green onions, cut into 1-inch slices

3 cups fresh broccoli florets, sliced

3 cups bok choy or Chinese cabbage, sliced diagonally into 1/2-inch pieces

2 tablespoons cornstarch, dissolved in 3 tablespoons of water

Stir together soy sauce, dry sherry, sesame oil, garlic, ginger, sugar, and sesame seeds to make marinade. Place chicken in a baking dish and pour marinade over it, then cover with plastic wrap and allow to marinate for at least 1 hour. Heat peanut oil over medium heat in a wok or skillet for 2 minutes. Add green onions, broccoli, and bok choy or cabbage. Stir-fry for 2 minutes, then remove from heat. Transfer to another dish and set aside. Place chicken pieces in wok or skillet and stir-fry for 3 to 5 minutes or until no longer pink in center. Remove chicken with a slotted spoon and place in a separate dish. Add cornstarch mixture to the wok or skillet and stir constantly over medium-high heat until it boils and thickens. Return chicken and vegetables to wok or skillet and stir constantly for 1 additional minute. Serve with rice or noodles. Yields 4 servings.

MakeOver Minute #42
ARMED AND READY

When you flex your faith, does it come across strong or wimpy? Consider two areas—the inner and the outer workings of your devotion to Christ. Like our upper arm muscles, which are made up of biceps (the inner muscle) and triceps (the outer muscle), you need to develop both your inner and outer faith muscles to shape up for life.

We strengthen and grow our inner faith by worshipping and getting to know God through prayer and Bible study. We exercise our outer faith by putting into practice what we've learned, both in the good times and the bad.

Since Christ suffered physical pain, you must arm yourselves with the same attitude he had, and be ready to suffer, too. For if you are willing to suffer for Christ, you have decided to stop sinning. And you won't spend the rest of your life chasing after evil desires, but you will be anxious to do the will of God.

—1 Peter 4:1-2 NLT

Prayer and Praise / Thankful Thoughts: _____

_____

_____

_____

Toned arms give you more than visual satisfaction. They help you perform routine daily activities—such as picking up children and carrying grocery bags—without the pain of muscle strain.

To develop well-defined arms, you'll need to work both your biceps and triceps using three- to five-pound hand weights. To get started, choose a weight with which you can perform three sets of 8 to 12 repetitions per arm, resting for only one minute between sets. You'll feel the burn when you start, but don't give up. Keep going, and the sting will subside as your arms get stronger. Just follow the program below to turn flabby to fabulous in only a few minutes a day.

- **Basic bicep curls:** Perform this exercise one arm at a time.

  1. Stand in an upright position with your shoulder blades squeezed together, feet shoulder-width apart, and knees slightly bent.

  2. Hold hand weights with an underhand grip, the palms of your hands facing forward and your arms hanging down at your sides.

  3. Flex at your elbows, curling your arms up until you bring the weight to shoulder level. Then, slowly lower your arm to the starting position.

- **Hammer bicep curls:** Perform this exercise one arm at a time.

  1. Stand in an upright position with your shoulder blades squeezed together, feet shoulder-width apart, and knees slightly bent.

  2. Grip the hand weight with the palms of your hands facing each other, your arms hanging down at your sides.

  3. Flex at your elbows, curling your arms up until the weight is at shoulder level. Slowly lower your arm to the starting position.

- **Overhead triceps lifts:** Perform this exercise one arm at a time.

  1. Sit in an upright position on the edge of a chair with your shoulder blades squeezed together and your abs tight, taking care not to arch your back.

  2. Grip the weights with your elbows flexed and the weights resting at shoulder level.

  3. Lift the weight over your head, positioning your elbow near your ear. Then, slowly lower your arm to the starting position.

- **Triceps push-ups:**

  1. Kneel on the floor and walk your hands out until your body forms a straight line from your head to your knees. Your hands should be directly beneath your shoulders.

  2. Pull your stomach in and tighten your abs.

  3. Slowly lower your body until your nose is three to four inches from the floor, then slowly return to the starting position.

Remember—always check with your physician before you start any exercise routine.

MakeOver Minute #43
THE BLUES

Feeling blue? You're not alone. According to recent studies, one out of every four women will experience a severe bout of depression in her lifetime.

When I was experiencing depression, the one thing that worked for me was to get the focus off myself and put my energy into helping others. Jesus said, "It is more blessed to give than to receive" (Acts 20:35 NKJV). Below are some other ideas to help you blow away the blues.

- **Write a psalm to God.** David openly expressed his hurts and concerns to God the Father: "Do not hide Your face from me; do not turn Your servant away in anger; You have been my help; do not leave me nor forsake me, O God of my salvation" (Psalm 27:9 NKJV).

- **Talk to someone.** Open up to a trusted friend, clergy member, or counselor, or join a support group. You need the love and support of others, as encouraged in Proverbs 24:6: "By wise counsel you will wage your own war, and in a multitude of counselors there is safety" (NKJV).

- **Give yourself permission to grieve**. The death of a loved one, the breakup of a relationship, the termination of a job, or any other loss needs to be grieved. Matthew 5:4 says, "Blessed are those who mourn, for they shall be comforted" (NKJV).

- **Think positive.** Discipline your mind to have a positive outlook about yourself, your life, and your future. Remember that "God not only loves you very much but also has put his hand on you for something special" (1 Thessalonians 1:4).

Dear friends, do not be surprised at the painful trial you are suffering, as though something strange were happening to you. But rejoice that you participate in the sufferings of Christ, so that you may be overjoyed when his glory is revealed.

—1 Peter 4:12-13 NIV

_____

_____

_____

Have you ever been on a fruitless quest to find the perfect pair of blue jeans? Did you leave the store feeling blue?

I've experienced years of trial and error in my own quest for great jeans, and I've discovered some true-blue shopping secrets for just about everybody. Here's how to find blue jeans that fit *and* are fit to be worn!

- **Pocket size and placement are the secret to your seat.** Smaller pockets will make your bottom look larger, lower pockets give it a boost, and if you have a flat bottom, choose jeans with embellished pockets.

- **Fit your shape.** Did you know that two women can be the exact same height and weight, yet wear different sizes of jeans because they don't have the same shape? Don't be a slave to trends. Choose a pair that's designed to flatter your shape, and you'll always be in style.

- If you want to **flatten your tummy,** try a dark-colored, medium- to high-rise pair of jeans that come no higher than your belly button.

- **Slim your hips** by avoiding jeans with slit pockets, which tend to pucker and draw attention to the hip area. Instead, opt for jeans without front pockets or with faux pockets.

- **Trim your thighs** by sticking with dark-colored jeans that are not too tight and flared styles that draw the eye down and away from your thigh area.

- **Look for denim that offers a bit of stretch,** which makes for both a flattering fit and comfortable wear.

- **Boot-cut and flared leg jeans create a long, lean look** that flatters most gals.

- **Avoid tapered legs** unless you are ultra-slim, as this type of fit makes your thighs and hips look larger.

- **Make sure your jeans are long enough** to cover the tops of your shoes. Too-short jeans make your legs look stubby and dumpy.

MakeOver Minute #44
BACK OFF

It's easy to allow a hurt to turn to bitterness without even realizing it. Like looking in a three-way mirror, we need to look behind us to see what we need to let go of.

After my son was born, I realized I was suppressing a grudge. A long-buried hate for my birth father welled up inside of me. You see, my birth father walked out on my mother and me when I was only three years old. It wasn't until I'd given birth to my own child that I wondered how anyone could abandon his own baby. I became consumed with a bitterness that was completely understandable but very self-destructive. As difficult as it was, I had to come to terms with the grudge monkey and get him off my back once and for all.

The first thing I had to do was remove the disguise and stop hiding the feelings I'd managed to block out. It was time to recognize and deal with the grudge.

The second step I had to take was to realize I couldn't handle it alone. I had to pray and ask God to help me forgive my birth father for abandoning me. Then, I had to ask Him to help me to love him and to pray for him. Matthew 5:44 really spoke to me: "I'm telling you to love your enemies. Let them bring out the best in you, not the worst. When someone gives you a hard time, respond with the energies of prayer."

As you look back in time, you're sure to discover some things worth remembering—such as the birth of a child—but remember that grudges aren't worth keeping. They need to be removed once and for all.

There is a time for everything...A time to search and a time to lose. A time to keep and a time to throw away.

—Ecclesiastes 3:1,6 NLT

Prayer and Praise / Thankful Thoughts: _____

_____

_____

_____

Most of us don't pay attention to what we can't see. It's not until you're in the dressing room, trying on clothes in front of a three-way mirror, that you catch a glimpse of your bulging backside. When properly strengthened and toned, your back muscles give you good posture, let you perform day-to-day tasks without back strain, and give you a well-defined rear view.

The following techniques will help you bare your best back.

- **Disguise:** Many of today's very clingy styles emphasize back folds. To help disguise this, wear a camisole or T-shirt containing spandex. This smooths the area and diminishes bulges. Also, make sure you're wearing the right bra size. Wearing the band lower on your back helps hide back fat.

- **Develop:** Diet is the answer to getting rid of fat, but exercise is the solution to getting rid of flab. The following exercises performed in two sets of 8 to 12 repetitions daily will yield visible results in just four to six weeks.

  1. **Roll back:** Stand with your back straight, feet shoulder-width apart, and knees slightly bent. Grip a three-to-five-pound weight in each hand. Keeping your back straight, bend 90 degrees from the waist, allowing your arms to hang down toward the floor with your palms facing your legs. Roll your shoulder blades together and bend your elbows, raising the weights up to the sides of your torso. Hold for a count of four, then lower for a count of four until you are back to your starting position.

  2. **Fly back:** Sit on the edge of a chair with your feet together and a three-to five-pound weight in each hand. Lean forward from the waist, allowing your arms to hang down next to your calves with your elbows slightly bent and your palms facing each other. Roll your shoulder blades together and raise your arms up to your sides until they are parallel with the floor. Pause for a count of four, then lower for a count of four until you are back to your starting position.

  3. **Row back:** Stand with your feet shoulder-width apart and your knees slightly bent. Hold a three- to five-pound weight in your right hand and lean forward, placing your left hand on your left thigh for support. Let your right arm hang down, then lift it until your hand is at waist level. Slowly lower the weight back to the starting position. After you have completed 8 to 12 repetitions, repeat this exercise with the left arm.

MakeOver Minute #45
DON'T MENTION IT

There's a dirty little secret with which many women are burdened but rarely mention. It's molestation, and whether or not it's affected you directly or indirectly, the humiliation of sexual abuse is something that silently burdens many women. It can provoke feelings of shock, shame, guilt, fear, anger, and depression. It can even cause the victim to question what she did to cause the person to violate her. She can go on and on wondering why she couldn't stop the abuse.

The first thing you must do to begin the healing process is come to terms with the fact that *you are not to blame*. What was done to you is *not* your fault! You are not responsible for the perpetrator's behavior. The second thing you need to do is talk about it. Stop the silence and get it out in the open so that you can end the ongoing effects of the emotional abuse associated with the incident. Sexual abuse is hard but not impossible to deal with. Below are answers to some very important questions I've been asked by victims of sexual abuse.

- **Will God forgive me?** God does not blame you for what happened to you. You are innocent. God loves you and wants you to forgive yourself.

   It is clear to us, friends, that God not only loves you very much but also has put his hand on you for something special.
   —1 Thessalonians 1:4

- **Must I forgive the perpetrator?** Forgiving the person who violated you helps you heal, but you cannot do this on your own. You need God's help to forgive the seemingly unforgivable.

   If you forgive others the wrongs they have done to you, your Father in heaven will also forgive you.
   —Matthew 6:14 GNT

- **Why did God let this happen to me?** God does not will evil on anybody—in fact, He abhors it. And even though He allows tragedy, He has no part in sin. Instead, God is there to pick up the pieces and rebuild your life from the inside out.

  We know that all things work together for good to those who love God, to those who are the called according to His purpose.

  —Romans 8:28 NKJV

- **How can I move past this and get on with my life?** Allow God to work in you and through you. It takes time, but it can be done—*all* things are possible with God.

  All praise to the God and Father of our Master, Jesus the Messiah! Father of all mercy! God of all healing counsel! He comes alongside us when we go through hard times, and before you know it, he brings us alongside someone else who is going through hard times so that we can be there for that person just as God was there for us.

  —2 Corinthians 1:3-4

Prayer and Praise / Thankful Thoughts: _____

_____

_____

_____

Have you ever noticed that some questions never get answered because they're never asked? There are some questions we feel dumb asking because they're just too personal—like questions regarding feminine issues. In case you were wondering, here are the answers to three of the most frequent questions that are never asked.

- **How can I control feminine itch?** This is actually a common problem. Feminine itch can be caused by a number of things—allergies to perfumes, lotions or soaps; intercourse; perspiration; wet swimsuit bottoms or panties; jeans that are too tight; vaginal dryness; scented toilet tissue; failure to wipe properly after urinating; yeast infections; sexually transmitted diseases; or even a woman's monthly menstrual cycle. If the previous suggestions don't point to a solution, you can try a number of over-the-counter ointments and creams, or you can add half a cup of baking soda to your bath and soak in it for ten minutes. If the itching still persists, consult your gynecologist.

- **My friend has vaginal odor. How can I tell her, and how can I help her?** You both might be a little embarrassed at first, but as a friend, how can you *not* tell her? Believe me—she'll be thankful you did. Many things can cause vaginal odor—menstruation, poor vaginal hygiene, leakage, or a vaginal infection. Cleaning yourself with a baby wipe and changing your pad or tampon more frequently throughout the course of the day can usually remedy vaginal odor caused by menstruation. Wearing a panty liner and changing it frequently may eliminate odor caused by leakage. Again, use a baby wipe to clean the area every time you change the liner. If you suspect the odor is caused by an infection, consult your gynecologist immediately. Some common signs of infection are—but are not limited to—vaginal discharge, itching, redness, and swelling.

- **When I cough, sneeze, or exercise, I experience urine leakage. Is this normal?** Yes, feminine leakage is very normal. In fact, the older you get, the more normal it becomes. You can do several things to help this problem. 1) Consult your doctor. 2) Wear panty liners or products made especially for this problem. 3) Kegel! I first learned about the Kegel pelvic exercise when I was pregnant, and I must say it really works! (The exercise is named after a Dr. Kegel, who invented it.) The muscles attached to your pelvic bone act like a hammock to hold in your pelvic organs. You can feel these muscles when you stop and start the flow of urine. Once you have located the muscles, simply tighten and relax them over and over, about a hundred times a day.

MakeOver Minute #46
INCOGNITO

God calls us to share with and care for one another, but we can't do that if we refuse to get real. It's all about humility—a willingness to open up and be vulnerable with each other for the purpose of help and healing.

All of you should be of one mind, full of sympathy toward each other, loving one another with tender hearts and humble minds.

—1 Peter 3:8 NLT

We need to stop worrying about what others will think and start giving them the opportunity to be thoughtful toward us. Pride and fear rob us of being blessed and rob others of giving us the blessing. Think about it from the perspective of the one doing the helping instead of the one being helped. Are you annoyed, put out, shocked, or appalled when someone reaches out to you for support? Not usually. Most of the time, we welcome the opportunity to serve God by serving others.

It's time to stop trying to appear picture-perfect and start being the real deal. Get honest with God, yourself, and others. Remember, we're all in the same boat. Each of us is faithfully trying to get through life and be better today than we were yesterday. That's all the more reason to share and care alike!

I don't mean to say that I have already achieved these things or that I have already reached perfection! But I keep working toward that day when I will finally be all that Christ Jesus saved me for and wants me to be.

—Philippians 3:12 NLT

Prayer and Praise / Thankful Thoughts: _____

_____

_____

_____

None of us are flawless. We all have something we'd like to change about our outward appearance. For you, it might be the size of your bustline, the color of your eyes, or the shape of your waist. Your trouble spot toys with your self-confidence, making you think, *If I only looked perfect like Paris Hilton, other people would like me better.* The fact is, if you were heir to the Hilton finances, you'd be able to fix just about any external issue too. The majority of us, though, don't fall into this category and need to find ways to disguise our disappointments on budgeted dollars. You *can* camouflage your not-so-flattering features and feel fabulous about the way you're put together. Let's start at the top and work our way down.

1. **Piercing eyes:** Some gals wish for sapphire blue, emerald green, or Liz Taylor–violet eyes. And with the help of colored contacts, it's possible to either enhance what you have or totally change the color altogether. Avoid matching your eye shadow to your eye color, but instead enhance your baby blues—or browns or greens—with a complementary color.

2. **Floppy arms:** Do you long to hide flabby, saggy, or pudgy arms? Simply wear long, flowing sleeves. Stay away from spaghetti straps, sleeveless tops, and cap sleeves.

3. **Busty or bustless:** Breasts come in all shapes and sizes—some small, others large—but all can look great with a little know-how. Enhance a flat chest with a high-neck or halter-style top. If you're well-endowed, wear lower, rounded necklines—but not so low that you expose yourself.

4. **Tummy troubles:** Flabby stomachs are easily camouflaged in wrap- or empire-style tops or dresses. Avoid wearing low-cut jeans or anything so tight it accentuates tummy overhang.

5. **Back blubber:** Rolls down the back are easily disguised with a Spandex-type camisole or T-shirt worn under your favorite top.

6. **In the rear:** Are you bottom-heavy or bottomless? Hide a large bottom with a flared jacket or shirt that covers the area. Perk up a flat bottom with large, embellished back pockets.

7. **Limited legs:** Visually lengthen legs by wearing all one color on your bottom half. Your pants or skirt, stockings, and shoes should all match. Pointed shoes also visually elongate the leg.

8. **Ample ankles:** Wear pants or long skirts with the same color stockings. Avoid capri pants, short skirts, and kitten heels.

MakeOver Minute #47
CURRENT EVENT

One of my high-school teachers always stressed the importance of staying on top of current events. Each week, he challenged us with an extra-credit assignment to read the newspaper every day and stay up-to-date on what was taking place in the world. This project not only inspired us to read the paper and discover new information daily, but also allowed us to intelligently discuss what we'd read.

Keeping up with the trends also pertains to conversation. So many witnessing opportunities arise in the course of an average conversation every single day. Current events generate questions that need answers. When tragedy strikes, people ask, "How could this happen?" If the weather is bizarre and unpredictable, people wonder why.

Current trends are the perfect segue into sharing biblical principles without being preachy. In fact, many times I've used current events to communicate basic values found in the book of Proverbs.

Stay up to date on the latest issues and use them to bring the Bible out of a time warp and make it relevant to those around you. Use current events to offer hope to those looking for answers.

Let your conversation be gracious and effective so that you will have the right answer for everyone.

—Colossians 4:6 NLT

Prayer and Praise / Thankful Thoughts: _____

_____

_____

_____

Are you caught in a time warp? When was the last time you updated your look? Staying up on the trends can be exhausting and expensive without indulging in a little savoir faire. You don't need a lot of money to stay current. You just need to know how to manage what you have and what you need.

First, if you want to update your look, what do you want to look like? Current fashions range from classic to comfortable to cute to commanding—all depending on how you wear them. Comfortable clothing follows the latest fashions but is made from easy-care fabrics, such as soft knits and cottons. Classic clothes sport the latest cuts in a more traditional tailored fashion. Cute clothing, however, is typically quite flashy and flamboyant. And commanding clothes demand attention and carry an air of authority about them. If you're not sure which look you prefer, flip through a current fashion magazine and single out what appeals to you. Remember—don't choose something just because it looks good on your favorite celebrity. Buy it only if *you* will wear it—and keep these tips in mind:

- **Shop smart.** Don't pay retail unnecessarily. Shop discount stores where you can save 50 percent or more off the suggested retail price.

- **Modernize your existing wardrobe** by adding new accessories—a trendy new necklace, eye-catching earrings, a beautiful belt, a fancy new hair accessory.

- **Add your own bling** to jeans, bags, and T-shirts. Beads, buttons, ribbons, and patches can bring new life to old styles. Shop your local craft store for ideas.

- **Make an appointment with your hair stylist** for a cool new cut and style. Search magazines for a hairdo that will look great on you, work with your hair type, and be easy to style once you get home.

- **Update your makeup** with new lipstick, nail polish, and eye shadow colors.

These are just a few ideas that you can try to create a brand-new, current you. Whether you try one or all, you can feel self-assured as you step out and strut your stuff in style!

MakeOver Minute #48
HIGH MAINTENANCE

Esther was the original Queen of High Maintenance. An orphaned Jewish woman, she was one of those selected to go to the palace of King Xerxes of Persia and be groomed as potential queen. For 12 months, Esther was given the prescribed royal beauty treatment for all of the queen hopefuls. At the end of the beauty regimen, she was brought before the king, who favored her and made her his new queen.

Meanwhile, Mordecai, a government official who had raised Esther, exposed an assassination plot against the king. Soon after that, a self-centered man named Haman became the prime minister. As the king's right-hand man, Haman demanded that everyone bow before him as he walked by. Mordecai, however, refused, which filled the prime minister with rage. When Haman discovered Mordecai was a Jew, he decided to destroy all of the Jews throughout Xerxes' kingdom. He even tricked the king himself into launching the evil plot.

Mordecai quickly sent a message to Queen Esther, alerting her to the plot against her people. Esther fasted and prayed, then came up with a plan to save her people. She asked the king and Haman to be special guests at a banquet she was hosting just for them. During the feast, Queen Esther found great favor with the king and he offered her anything she wanted—up to half of the kingdom. She simply requested that her guests join her for a second banquet the next day.

That night, the king couldn't sleep. He began to read through the royal history books, and his attention was brought to the assassination plot Mordecai had foiled. As he read, he noticed that Mordecai had never been rewarded for his heroic effort, so he went to Haman to inquire of the proper way to honor such a loyal subject. Now, Haman, being the conceited guy he was, thought the king was referring to *him,* so he suggested an elaborate reward. The king approved and, of course, Haman was shocked to discover that his enemy Mordecai was to receive the favor of the king.

Later that day at the second banquet, the king again asked Queen Esther what she wanted—up to half of his kingdom. This time, she revealed Haman's evil plot to kill the Jews and asked that he spare her people. The king immediately assented and ordered Haman to be hung. This is the story of Esther, the high-maintenance queen, who had been appointed for "just such a time as this" (Esther 4:14).

Prayer and Praise / Thankful Thoughts: _____

_____

_____

_____

The term *high maintenance* typically describes someone who requires a lot of attention in order to function properly or stay pleased. It usually refers to how much time you put into yourself, or how much time others have to put into you. You know you're high maintenance if...

- you frequent the cosmetic department looking for the latest and greatest miracle product.
- you're more dedicated to keeping your manicure appointments than your annual physicals.
- you wake up at 6 a.m. to be ready for that special event at 7 p.m.
- you can't pass a mirror without checking in.
- you classify a blemish as an emergency and give it urgent care.
- you own at least a half-dozen pairs of black shoes and still need another pair.
- having an audience doesn't bother you a bit—in fact, you crave it!
- emotional support always outweighs the need for support hose.

Being high maintenance isn't really such a bad thing *unless* you let it interfere with other important priorities. If being high maintenance means being selfish and self-centered, then you need to get over yourself and realize it's not all about you.

Balance the time you spend on yourself with the time you spend on others. Treat a friend to lunch and let *her* do the majority of the talking. Spend some time with your mom by pampering yourselves with a mother–daughter pedicure. Give a sincere compliment to a colleague without expecting anything in return. Make others a priority, and you'll maintain a high quality of life.

MakeOver Minute #49
CHOCOLATE IS LIFE

"My momma always said life was like a box of chocolates. You never know what you're gonna get." This is one of the most memorable quotes from the hit movie *Forrest Gump*. I'd never thought of this before then, but how true it is!

When I was a little girl, my auntie always shared her box of chocolates with me. I would gaze wide-eyed at the large assortment, wondering what was inside each one of those tiny chocolate-covered surprises. My favorites were the toffee and the caramel, and—like a kid at Christmas—I always hoped I'd get what I wanted. Of course, I was terribly disappointed if I didn't!

Life is like a box of chocolates—loaded with surprises, some delightful and some downright disagreeable. The yummy ones, of course, are easy to swallow, but the yucky ones are hard to stomach. Those yucky ones, however, determine our depth of character. If life were all good and your faith was never challenged, where would you be spiritually? It's the bad times that test our faith and cause us to mature as we learn to rely on God through everything we endure.

When the going gets tough, we sometimes open a box of chocolates looking for comfort. In fact, we often turn to addictive things such as food, alcohol, drugs, or shopping—anything to dull the pain we feel inside. We forget to rely on the Spirit of God, who is living in us, to get us through the distasteful portions of our lives.

> *Do not get drunk with wine, which will only ruin you; instead, be filled with the Spirit.*
>
> —Ephesians 5:18 GNT

Girlfriend, life is like a box of chocolates. You never know what it's going to dish out, but through it all God will help you remain levelheaded and delight you with guilt-free comfort when you indulge in His Spirit.

If chocolate is your life, you're about to be in for a sweet treat. Have you ever dreamed of basking guilt-free in chocolate without worrying about weight gain? If so, light a chocolate-scented candle, grab a mug of cocoa, and indulge yourself in the decadent delights below.

- **Chocolate face mask:** This self-indulgent face mask is an excellent moisturizer for normal skin. Mix together one-third cup cocoa powder, one-quarter cup honey, three tablespoons heavy cream, three tablespoons oatmeal, and two teaspoons cottage cheese. Gently smooth onto your face, avoiding the eye area. Relax for 15 minutes, then thoroughly rinse off with warm water.

- **Chocolaty bubble bath:** Inspired by Hershey, this decadent bath delivers when eating chocolate alone just isn't enough. Mix one-eighth cup unsweetened cocoa powder and one-third cup nonfat instant dry milk together and sprinkle into bath while water is still running. Add one-half cup unscented bubble bath and stir with hand. Climb in, relax, and savor!

- **Hot-chocolate pedicure:** Pamper your tootsies with this sweet and indulgent chocolate foot bath. Mix together three tablespoons unsweetened cocoa powder and three tablespoons nonfat instant dry milk, then set aside. Next, mix together three tablespoons sugar, one teaspoon cinnamon, one teaspoon nutmeg, and two tablespoons peppermint oil to create an exfoliating paste. Fill pedicure tub with hot (but not too hot!) water and add cocoa mixture. Soak your feet for ten minutes, then exfoliate with the sugar mix. Rinse thoroughly, then smooth on cocoa butter.

MakeOver Minute #50
FIXER-UPPER

Our outer beauty is fixed on what we can visibly see, but our inner beauty is fixed on what isn't visible to the human eye.

GOD judges persons differently than humans do. Men and women look at the face; GOD looks into the heart.

—1 Samuel 16:7

Too often, we get so caught up with keeping up appearances that fixing our faces becomes more important than fixing our lives. Our makeup mishaps get immediate attention, but our moral mistakes are often trivialized or ignored altogether. *If no one else notices*, we figure, *why get anxious?*

Take time to fix the inside. Whatever it is, make it right. If you need to apologize, do it. If you need to return something that doesn't belong to you, give it back. If you need to be honest, stop lying and start telling the truth. Don't wait any longer to fix up what lies beneath the surface. God doesn't care if you wear too much perfume, but He does detest the stench of sin.

God's eyes are fixed on you, so fix your attention on Him. Turn away from evil, and replace evil with good. Make fixing up the inside your top priority, and you'll always be at peace with God.

We fix our eyes not on what is seen, but on what is unseen. For what is seen is temporary, but what is unseen is eternal.

—2 Corinthians 4:18 NIV

Prayer and Praise / Thankful Thoughts: _____

_____

_____

_____

Have you ever accidentally overdosed on perfume or overdone it with the blusher? Well, don't panic! Some simple fixer-uppers can undo the most common beauty blunders quickly and easily so you can continue the process without having to start from scratch.

- Did you stay out too late and wake up with red eyes and dark under-eye circles? Not to worry. Apply a couple of eyedrops formulated especially for red-eye, then wait two minutes. Next, gently apply concealer under each eye, allowing it to dry for five minutes before you blend it in.

- If you discover you have a makeup line, dab some moisturizer on a spongy makeup wedge and gently blend the make-up into your jawline or hairline.

- The next time you end up with clown cheeks, dip the flat end of a spongy makeup wedge into loose powder, gently tap it to remove the excess, then use it to blend in your blusher.

- If you get your eyeliner or lip liner out of line, use the narrow end of a spongy makeup wedge to realign it.

- The next time you overtweeze your brows, use a brow brush to brush the hairs in the opposite direction of growth so the bare spot becomes visible. Next, use a well-sharpened brow pencil to fill in the gap with light, feathery strokes. Brush your brows back into place.

- If your eye shadow is too intense, gently tone it down by rolling a cotton swab over the area.

- Are your lashes clumping together? Keep an old mascara wand from a used-up tube, clean it, and save it for such a time as this. A mascara-free wand will remove the clump instead of adding to it.

- Does your face look too powdery? Pour bottled water into an atomizer, hold it eight inches from your face, and spray twice. Gently pat dry with a tissue, being careful not to rub your face as you pat it.

- Is your lip color lacking? Try blending two or three colors together to get that perfect match.

- Did you put on too much perfume? Use an unscented baby wipe to wipe away the excess.

MakeOver Minute #51
TAILOR-MADE

God created man in his own image, in the image of God he
created him; male and female he created them.

—Genesis 1:27 NIV

We were tailor-made in the image of God, created for His glory.

God has made us what we are. In Christ Jesus,
God made us to do good works, which God planned in
advance for us to live our lives doing.

—Ephesians 2:10 NCV

Although each one of us is unique, we're all created in the image of God and for the sole purpose of loving, obeying, and serving Him to the best of our abilities. Yet many of us see ourselves as misfits, wondering how we could possibly serve God with our seeming lack of skill or less-than-perfect past. Sister—you're not alone! The Bible is filled with ordinary, no-talent, sinful people whom God used despite themselves. Take Moses, for instance—he stuttered. Rahab was a prostitute. David was a murderer. And who could forget Jonah? He ended up as fish vomit! Then there was Peter—a disciple of Christ who denied Him three times. Mary Magdalene was demon-possessed. And Lazarus—he was dead! Now, if God can use them, He certainly can use you!

God is glorified when we allow Him to work through our weaknesses.

My grace is sufficient for you, for my power is made perfect in
weakness. Therefore I will boast all the more gladly about my
weaknesses, so that Christ's power may rest on me.

—2 Corinthians 12:9 NIV

God made you just the way you are, and it makes Him happy when you serve Him through your own unique capabilities. But remember—you are responsible for doing something with what you have. So don't sit around waiting for something better to come along. Glorify God with what you've got.

I've always been interested in makeup and fashion, and nearly every report card I ever received had the same comments in the conduct column: "Tammy tends to talk too much." I overlooked these abilities for years, not realizing God could use them for His glory. But here I am, teaching women everywhere to be beautiful from the inside out. Don't be tempted to think that what you do and who you are is insignificant, because God doesn't make mistakes. You are accountable to serve God with what you've been given.

What do the words *availability, accountability, capability,* and *responsibility* have in common? *A-bility!* God has custom-fit you, and He'll enable you to accomplish His purpose for you. You just need to make yourself available.

Now you're dressed in a new wardrobe. Every item of your new way of life is custom-made by the Creator, with his label on it. All the old fashions are now obsolete.

—Colossians 3:10

Prayer and Praise / Thankful Thoughts: _____

_____

_____

_____

One of the best but most commonly overlooked wardrobe resources is tailoring. A good tailor is extremely beneficial, saving you both time and money. An expert tailor can make an old outfit look new or make an inexpensive outfit look high-priced just with a few nips and tucks. I've owned one fairly expensive suit for years that I didn't want to give up just because it had gone out of style. I took it to the tailor and had it made over from top to bottom. It now looks brand-new, and it only cost me $35. That's a fraction of the cost of a new suit!

Some stores will alter garments for free, while others charge a nominal fee. Whatever the cost, factor it in, because it's well worth the outcome. Even if you purchase something where altering is not available, you can always have it tailored. For example, I bought an adorable dress off the clearance rack at TJ Maxx, for only $14. It was a bit large on me, so I paid a seamstress $10 to custom fit it. Now, it looks like a million bucks!

When you're having clothing items altered, keep these simple tips in mind:

- Hems should never hit at the widest part of your calf. Shortening or lengthening them by just half an inch or so can be the difference between appearing tubby and looking trim.

- Tapering a skirt instantly makes you look ten pounds thinner.

- Jackets should never stop at the widest part of your hip, rump, or thigh.

- Jackets should hang straight from the shoulder to the hem without bunching up or pulling across the bustline, back, belly, or hips.

- Shoulder seams on a jacket should extend one-quarter to one-half inch past the tip of your shoulder line, unless the jacket is a drop-shoulder style or has raglan sleeves that extend from the collar to the wrist.

- Jackets should have ample room in the shoulders, elbows, backs, and sleeves so you can easily move your arms.

- Jacket sleeves should just cover your wrist bone.

- When you button your jacket, it should not pucker, and the lapels should lie flat.

Tailor-made clothing is well worth the effort! A little alteration can give almost any garment a polished flair without an inflated price tag. The next time you find an outfit you really like at a great price that doesn't fit you quite right, see if the store offers altering. If not, inquire about the return policy. If the item can be returned, take it to your tailor—with the tags still on—and get a professional opinion. If it can be custom fit, great! If not, simply return it to the store with the tags intact, unaltered and with the original sales receipt.

MakeOver Minute #52
NEW YOU RESOLUTIONS

Recently, I ran across a commitment card from the year 2001. On it I had resolved to pray and read my Bible more thoroughly and remember all of my nieces' and nephews' birthdays. Now, these might not sound like very aggressive goals to you, but they were some pretty big challenges for me!

I had to make some advance preparations. The first thing I did was orchestrate a plan that involved starting a prayer diary, setting a Bible-reading goal (reading through the Old Testament), and stocking up on birthday cards. The diary allowed me to stay focused, the biblical goal kept me on track, and the birthday cards—which I stamped and preaddressed—made sure I was ready. "No more excuses," became my motto. When I truly committed not only to my convictions but to changing my actions as well, it worked!

When you're ready to resolve, it's important to keep a few things in mind:

- **Keep your eyes open.** The enemy desperately tries to distract you from accomplishing your goals so he can make you feel like a failure. I once realized my prayer life was suffering because whenever I'd sit down to pray, the phone would ring or I'd think of some task that needed to be done. I remedied the distraction by turning off the telephone ringer and quickly jotting down a to-do list in the margin of my prayer diary.

- **Hold onto your convictions**. Stay focused on your goal. It's *your* convictions that will enable you to change, and that change will help you remain committed to the cause. I'm convicted to know God better through His Word, which has changed me from the inside out and made me even more determined in the process.

- **Give it all you've got.** You *will* have those days when you fail to meet the standard, but don't let that discourage you from picking up where you left off. Sometimes I forgot to mail the birthday cards in a timely manner, so I had to send them out late. At least they eventually arrived!

So make a new resolution to commit to those things that matter most to God, and your convictions will yield change for the better.

Hold tight to your convictions, give it all you've got, be resolute.

—1 Corinthians 16:13

Prayer and Praise / Thankful Thoughts: _____

_____

_____

_____

I'd like to spend more time with family and friends. I vow to exercise more and eat less. I want to quit smoking. I'd like to stress less and enjoy life more. This is the year I really need to get out of debt. Once and for all, I'm going to clean things out and get organized. I'm definitely going to volunteer this year.

Do any of these common New Year's resolutions sound familiar to you?

Year after year, it's the same old thing—we make resolutions in hopes of changing our lives for the better, but we rarely stick with them for more than two or three weeks. The problem is, our basic strategy is to commit to our conviction *without* committing to change.

Now, our intentions are good. But our method of setting the goal and then going for it rarely works because we forget to *strategize*. We fail to plan how we're going to perform the task and how we will persevere through unexpected interruptions—interruptions that usually cause us to give up. For example, if weight loss is your goal, you need to plan what you will eat ahead of time so you're not tempted to eat what you shouldn't. You also need to have a backup plan in order to persevere through the setbacks.

The key to keeping any resolution is flexibility. Resolutions are not accomplished overnight. They are simply a starting point—a declaration of the change you're going to make in your life. So prepare to alter your goals and readjust your plans as time passes and circumstances change.

Most of all, celebrate your successes—no matter how great or small— keep your eyes open for obstacles, hold on to your convictions, give it all you've got, and never, ever give up.

If at first you don't succeed, try, try again.

—Thomas H. Palmer

MakeOver Minute #53
HUNGER PAINS

Many people think that life is all about satisfying their own insatiable appetites. They might hunger for more money, a bigger house, a nicer car, or lavish vacations—anything that gratifies their longings for "the good life," but what they don't realize is that these things, like snack food, only fill you up temporarily before you are craving more.

In Deuteronomy 8:3, Moses teaches us that life is not about what we stuff our live with, but instead, what we hide in our hearts.

*Thy word have I hid in mine heart, that I might
not sin against thee.*
—Psalm 119:11 KJV

Memorizing Scripture is an effective deterrent against sin. When Satan tempted Jesus to turn stones into bread, Jesus quoted Deuteronomy 8:3— "Man does not live by bread alone but on every word that comes from the mouth of the LORD"—to indicate that inner strength is not drawn from a balanced diet but instead from an in-depth relationship with God.

Knowing, memorizing, and obeying Scripture are important steps to skillfully resisting Satan's attacks during spiritual combat. Knowing the Bible gives you spiritual understanding. Memorizing Scripture equips you for spiritual warfare. And being obedient demonstrates your spirituality *and* sets you apart. After all, even Satan knows and can quote the Bible.

Know it. Memorize it. Obey it. Satisfy your hunger for the Word of God, and hide it in your heart so you won't be tempted to sin against God.

Prayer and Praise / Thankful Thoughts: _____

_____

_____

_____

Hunger pains can sure be vicious when they hit! One minute, you're fine. The next minute, you need something to scarf down ASAP—which isn't necessarily a bad thing unless you're not prepared. It's junk food that gives snacking a bad rap. The fact is, snack attacks are okay as long as you snack smart and remember that skillful snacking involves eating *only* when you're truly hungry.

Healthful snacking encourages healthy living. Well-chosen snacks help you not only manage your hunger pains, but your weight and energy level as well. The following steps to successful snacking can eliminate hunger pains with minimal effort.

- **Snack log:** Write down when you eat and what you eat. Keeping a snack log forces you to acknowledge what you're eating so you can objectively evaluate your snacking habits.

- **Snack strategy:** Plan ahead to keep a variety of tasty, nutritious snacks at home, at work, or even in your car. Be prepared when hunger pains kick in so you're not tempted to give in to eating junk.

- **Snack habits:** As hard as it might seem, change your snacking habits. Don't snack out of boredom when you're mindlessly watching television or when you're studying. Snack only when you're hungry, and pay close attention to what—and how much of it—you're eating.

- **Snack substitutes:** Do you crave specifics when you snack, such as foods that are salty, crunchy, or sweet? Find healthy substitutes to satisfy your cravings.

- **Snack power:** Need a boost? A protein-filled snack will increase your energy level and suppress your appetite for a longer period of time.

- **Snack singles:** Measure and pre-package snacks in advance so you're not tempted to overdo it when a snack attack strikes.

- **Snack treats:** It's okay to satisfy overwhelming snacking indulgences from time to time, but don't overdo it. When you just *have* to eat a chocolate bar, try a handful of semi-sweet chocolate chips instead.

MakeOver Minute #54
DOIN' THAT THING YOU DO

The human body has many parts, but the many parts make up only one body. So it is with the body of Christ...God made our bodies with many parts, and he has put each part just where he wants it...In fact, some of the parts that seem weakest and least important are really the most necessary.

—1 Corinthians 12:12,14,18,22 NLT

In this portion of Scripture, Paul compares the body of Christ to a human body. Each part of your body has a different function to perform. One part doesn't outdo another—all are necessary to make it function properly. This is also true of the body of Christ—all the members must work together to be effective. Each part is essential, and no part is more esteemed than another in the eyes of the Lord. God expects each of us to use what we've been given to honor and glorify Him to the best of our ability. The problem is, we often become envious or arrogant in the process. We're either like the foot, moaning about our disabilities, or we're like the eye, bragging about our capabilities. Yet if your feet ran without looking or your eyes saw where they wanted to go but had no way to walk there, life would be pretty difficult.

So celebrate your place in the body of Christ. Be thrilled with your strengths, and disregard your weaknesses. Not everyone can play the keyboard and not everyone can lead a Bible study, but I guarantee that you can do *something*. There is not one gift that's needed more than another or one talent that overshadows another. If everyone preached, who would listen? If everyone cared for the babies in the nursery, who would disciple the youth? God gave each of us different talents, gathered us from diverse backgrounds, and united us in faith in Christ with the purpose of serving Him and supporting one another. So have confidence in your God-given ability, and stop comparing yourself to others.

You are Christ's body—that's who you are! You must never forget this. Only as you accept your part of that body does your "part" mean anything.

—1 Corinthians 12:27

_____

_____

_____

Work on what you do well, and don't worry about the things you don't do as well. Too often, we try to do things we're not good at just because we have something to prove.

I'm horrible at math, and I hate balancing my checkbook, but when I got married, I was told that all good wives balance their checkbooks. So that's what I set out to do. The first month balanced, but the second month was off by two dollars. I figured and I refigured and I just could not figure out where I went wrong. I spent hours going through canceled checks, digging for receipts, and telephoning the bank, but no matter how I counted, it just wouldn't add up. I was in tears when my husband walked in wondering what was wrong. Through the sobs, I sniffled out, "I want to be a good wife and I can't add!" My husband lovingly reassured me he had not married me for my math skills, and after that I never worried about balancing the checkbook again. Instead, I invested my time in cooking, which I love and am pretty good at, even if I do say so myself! Stick with what you're good at, and don't beat yourself up for what you're not.

God created each us with differing interests and varying talents. What interests you may not interest me, and my natural talents and abilities may be difficult for you to accomplish. So why do we waste so much time trying to be somebody else? Now, I'm not suggesting it's a bad idea to study and learn new things. What I'm saying is, don't try to be something you're not. Develop what you've been given.

John Maxwell said, "Find your passion and never work a day in your life."

How true it is! When you go with what you've been given, you are much more likely to succeed. Celebrate your uniqueness! Work with what you've got, and stop wasting time on what you're not. Live life to the fullest by pursuing your passion and growing in your area of giftedness.

MakeOver Minute #55
FEAR FACTOR

The story of David and Goliath provides an inspirational illustration of how confidence can overshadow fear (see 1 Samuel 17). Here, a young shepherd boy wasn't intimidated by a nine-foot giant because his faith in God was bigger than his fear of man. Most of us only fantasize about having boldness such as this. Our lives are often controlled by fear, and confronting the anxiety of the unknown is the biggest giant we'll ever face.

Fear can either immobilize you or ignite your faith. In the above story, when King Saul's forces were confronted by the giant, the entire army became frozen with fear. Verse 11 says, "They were terrified and deeply shaken" (NLT), which brings us to verse 12, when David enters the scene. The Bible describes the shepherd boy as small in stature but large in faith. In fact, just before he threw the giant to the ground, he shouted, "The battle is the LORD's and He will give you into our hands!"

David faced fear by depending on God. He knew that God was ultimately in control. He believed in the sovereignty of the Almighty, and knew that the outcome—whether good or bad—was in God's hands.

The absence of fear is found in God-confidence. It's all about knowing God on a more intimate level and understanding the attributes of His character. You'll be able to carry out His call with the assurance He will be with you every step of the way. You are never alone. Like David, you and God together are the majority, greater than any army of fear.

If God is for us, who [or what] can ever be against us?
—Romans 8:31 NLT

Prayer and Praise / Thankful Thoughts: _____

_____

_____

_____

So many people are plagued with fear—fear of everything from failing to flying. Sometimes these fears are rational and other times they're not, but that doesn't make them any less real to the people who are tortured by them. Living in fear is like having a debilitating disease that cripples our emotions and actions. Although fear plagues each one of us at some time or another, it doesn't paralyze everyone. The question is, *Why*? Why do some people live in fear, while others seem to outlive it?

It takes an extraordinary amount of strength, courage, and resilience to confront fear, and although we will never completely eliminate it from our lives, we *can* overcome it. Fearlessness is not the absence of fear but the ability to act in spite of it. When you're fearless, you're at the point where fear does not stop you from taking risks. You are able to try things without allowing the consequences of failure to stifle you.

Confidence is the opposite of fear. Confidence allows you to step out of your comfort zone and face life with boldness. When you live confidently, you can reach new heights that you once thought were beyond your grasp.

To diminish fear, you must face this giant head-on. Look at your fear in an objective manner, then use logic to defuse it. For instance, let's take a look at one of the most common fears—public speaking. First, realize that speaking in public won't kill you. You might feel like you want to die but, realistically, it's safe. Second, know your stuff. Advance training and preparation will get you ready to face the challenge. Third, practice. Courage always grows with practice.

Fear of failure is a state of mind. Change your thinking and change your perspective. Remember, fearlessness is fear wrapped in courage and delivered with an element of confidence.

MakeOver Minute #56
WALK IT OFF

Just the other day, my husband and I went for a walk into the woods. We got about two miles into the forest, when the sky grew dark, the heavens opened up, and torrential rains poured down. We turned around to head back, but we could hardly see a thing. Between the blinding rain, the thick forest, and dark cloud cover, we had only enough light to see what was directly in front of us. We held on to each other, trying to keep our footing, avoid the pitfalls, and stay on the right path until we were safely out of the woods and back home.

Life is much the same way. Stumbling blocks are everywhere. They loom in the darkness, just waiting to trip us up and throw us off course when we least expect it. And these hurdles come in many different forms—an unfaithful spouse, a troubled teen, a job layoff—all of which leave you wondering how to keep going and which way to turn.

Trust in the LORD with all your heart, and lean not on your own understanding; in all your ways acknowledge Him, and He shall direct your paths.
—Proverbs 3:5-6 NKJV

Look to God, and He will lead, guide, and direct you through every day of your life. He will be your own personal GPS (*God Provides Support*). Your Father will support you when you trip, pick you up when you fall, and comfort you when you get hurt. Trust in God, and you will find the way.

As you walk—and sometimes run—through life, you must faithfully trust God to lead you around the pitfalls and down the right path until you make it safely to your heavenly home.

Listen for GOD's voice in everything you do, everywhere you go; he's the one who will keep you on track.
—Proverbs 3:6

Prayer and Praise / Thankful Thoughts: _____

_____

_____

_____

Walking is a terrific weight-loss exercise. When you raise your heart rate by walking at a brisk, heart-pumping pace, you burn fat, slim down, and tone up. Walking has also been shown to reduce stress, promote a healthy heart, lower blood pressure, and lower cholesterol.

Before you start walking—or doing any other exercise—you should check with your doctor to make sure the physical exertion will help and not harm you. The other thing you will want to do is invest in a good pair of walking shoes. Buy shoes that have good arch support and fit properly when you're wearing athletic socks. Try both shoes on, and walk around the store before you buy them.

To maximize the benefits of healthful walking, you need to walk faster, longer, and on a regular basis. If you've never walked before, start out slow but steady and try to walk for at least 10 minutes a day, with the goal of increasing the time a little each week until you reach a full 30 minutes.

When you walk, maintain good, tall posture by keeping your chin parallel with the ground, your eyes on the horizon, and your shoulders back, being careful not to lean too far forward or backward. Keep your elbows at a 90-degree angle and pump your arms in such a way that your wrist moves from your chest to your waist in harmony with your pace. Walk more efficiently by shortening your stride and placing your heel down first so you can push off, which will increase your speed.

Make walking fun by keeping it interesting! If you're getting bored, map out a new route. Drive to another neighborhood to walk, or visit your local state park and hike down a scenic trail. If the treadmill's getting monotonous, turn on the television, crank up the tunes, or listen to a book on tape. I've actually used my time on the treadmill to learn some Chinese.

So walk it off. It takes an average of 10,000 steps a day to maintain weight and roughly 12,000 to 15,000 daily steps to lose weight. Lace up your sneakers, grab a pedometer if you wish, and make every step count!

MakeOver Minute #57
BLAH BUSTERS

Believer blahs have an ill effect on Christians. They make us lack care, compassion, and concern for one another and the things that are going on around us.

Observe how Christ loved us. His love was not cautious but extravagant. He didn't love in order to get something from us but to give everything of himself to us. Love like that.

—Ephesians 5:2

Self-sacrificing love is the best way to remedy faith that is in a funk. Here are some of my favorite ways to keep faith fresh:

- **Make love an action verb.** Don't just say you love others—show it! Find ways to reach out to other people, both those you know and those you don't. When my children were younger, we treated ourselves to ice cream once a week. Each week on our way to the ice-cream shop, we passed an elderly homeless man. Every week, the kids commented that we should help him, so we started to do just that. Once we brought him dinner, and another time we stuffed a backpack with goodies, including a Bible, and gave it to him. This was not only a great lesson for my kids, but it taught me something too—when you help others, you feel better about yourself.

- **Share your concerns**. Volunteer your time in an area that matters to you. Homeless shelters need help serving food, crisis pregnancy centers need counselors, and politicians need supporters to post signs. Whatever your care or concern, use it as a driving force to get involved.

Don't be complacent in your faith. Celebrate it. Be thankful you are allowed to live it, display it, and proclaim it. Not everyone is that fortunate. Some political regimes persecute—and even kill—believers. Never take your faith for granted. Get involved. Be compassionate, caring, and concerned, and you'll never fail to make a change.

Prayer and Praise / Thankful Thoughts: _____

_____

_____

_____

Ever have one of those days when you're in a funk and feeling blah? Nothing seems to excite you. You want to eat something, but you don't know what. You'd like to go somewhere, but don't know where. You'd love to call someone, but you never feel like talking when you're in one of these moods. Restlessness is no fun, and it can even make you feel depressed if you don't overcome it. It's time to learn how to beat the blahs!

- **Get moving.** As much as you might dread it, exercise is the best way to bust the blahs. Walking, in particular, will turn you from glum to glad when you get outside and clear your head.

- **Make a date.** Plan a get-together with your best friend, but don't fill her in on the details—make it a surprise. Planning a special treat for someone else gets your mind off yourself *and* gives you something to look forward to. Marriage blahs in particular could use some spice, and it's never too late for some zing. Plan a getaway with your hubby. It doesn't have to be expensive or far away—just use your imagination and make a memory.

- **Eat up.** Mother always told you to eat your fruits and veggies, and Mother was right. Fruits, vegetables, and whole grains raise your body's serotonin level, which elevates your feeling of well-being. Stress, in particular, can deplete serotonin reserves and cause energy levels to plummet as well as cause bouts of depression. "Stressed" spelled backwards is "desserts," and what better way to pick yourself up than with a yummy treat now and then.

- **Do something you enjoy.** If you love to sing, dance, or shop, just do it! I have a friend who loves to color, so when she's feeling blah, she pulls out her coloring book and crayons and does what makes her happy.

- **Write it down.** Sometimes the blahs make us introspective, so take the time to journal those thoughts. Many times God uses occasions such as these to get our attention, and we don't want to miss what He has to say. So grab a pen and paper, and reflect on His Word.

MakeOver Minute #58
MAKE IT COUNT

As I've gotten older, I've learned to stop investing my time and energy in things that don't matter. And I've learned to use what time and energy I do have more wisely.

During the time my mother was in ICU at the hospital, a gentleman in the room next door was on his deathbed. When the nurses asked the man what they could do to make him more comfortable, he asked them to call his son. I first met the son, his wife, and their two children in the waiting room outside the ICU corridor. They had just returned from visiting the severely ill gentleman and were weeping. I asked, "Is everything okay?" and the son smiled and said, "Yes, it's better than okay. My father just prayed to receive Christ." He went on to tell me that prior to this, his father had not spoken to him for years because of a disagreement. It took his dad being on his deathbed to get him to make amends with his son. He had also never met his grandchildren before. He told them he was sorry he had missed out on knowing them, and they told him that it was okay because, through Christ, they could all spend eternity together. The gentleman passed away soon after that, but the last days of his life taught an important message—it's never too late to get things right.

This is a hard lesson to learn. I wish I'd listened when older women advised me to cherish the time I spent with my young children. The days seemed endless to a young mom dealing with potty training, toddler energy, and general chaos. Now, there are times I wish I could go back to those days. I wouldn't worry about the dirty dishes in the sink, the piles of unwashed laundry, or the dirty handprints on the wall. I'd just sit down in the midst of the mess and make memories with my little ones over another game of Candy Land.

Your life is but a vapor. Don't allow the time to evaporate without making it count for the ones who count most to you.

What is your life? It is even a vapor that appears for a little time and then vanishes away.

—James 4:14 NKJV

_____

_____

_____

It seems that I'm forever trying to stretch every moment out of every day in order to get things done. I'm almost always working on two tasks at once in order to stay ahead. I tidy up my bedroom while I brush my teeth, dust while I'm on the phone, and keep up with the dishes while I cook. In fact, I'm even doing laundry as I write about this topic. Multitasking is a way of life.

I talk to women all the time who want more hours in their day. Most want time to do things they never have time for, such as exercise. Well, listen up all you multitaskers—I've got good news for you. You *can* make the most mundane chores count—count the loss of calories, that is!

Did you know that you can burn calories by performing everyday chores? Review the time required to burn 100 calories on the following list, and get busy. Oh, and though you can't necessarily burn double the calories by performing two chores at once, you *can* burn more if you work longer.

Lose 100 calories, more or less, in...

- **20 minutes** by trimming shrubs, weeding the garden, raking leaves, bagging leaves, cleaning rain gutters, washing windows.

- **25 minutes** by vacuuming, washing dishes, mopping, picking up toys, cleaning bathrooms, cleaning outdoor furniture.

- **30 minutes** by painting or wallpapering a room, washing the car, sweeping, washing the dog.

- **35 minutes** by dusting, preparing a meal (including setting the table), clearing the table, washing pots and pans.

- **40 minutes** by ironing, folding and putting away laundry, grocery shopping.

MakeOver Minute #59
OUTFITTED IN PERSONALITY

There are four basic personality types—*sanguine, melancholy, choleric,* and *phlegmatic*. Each can be identified by its own set of strengths and weaknesses. The strengths are the things we're naturally good at. The weaknesses are the strengths carried to extremes, which can become a hindrance instead of a help.

Below is a brief description of each personality type. See which one best fits you. (If this topic intrigues you, I highly recommend the book *Personality Plus by* Florence Littauer.)

- **Sanguine:** The number-one goal of this gal is to have fun! She's the life of the party, loves to talk, and has a great sense of humor. On the downside, she tends to exaggerate, forgets her obligations, and has an overwhelming need to be the center of attention.

- **Melancholy:** This gal is forever in search of perfection. She loves schedules, organization, details, and high standards. On the flip side, she can be moody, withdrawn, and self-deprecating.

- **Choleric:** This strong gal seeks control. She's drawn to leadership, and she's dynamic, decisive, and rarely discouraged. On the other hand, she tends to be bossy, demanding, unsympathetic, and a fanatical workaholic.

- **Phlegmatic:** Peace is what appeals most to this calm gal. She's cool, collected, competent, and steady, and she's excellent at mediating problems. In contrast, she can avoid responsibility, lack self-motivation, be unenthusiastic, and resist change.

When we learn to recognize ourselves, we can work on keeping our strengths in check so they don't become our weaknesses. And we can focus on being at our best for God.

Thank you for making me so wonderfully complex! Your workmanship is marvelous—and how well I know it.

—Psalm 139:14 NLT

Prayer and Praise / Thankful Thoughts: _____

_____

_____

_____

Did you know your preferred method of dress speaks volumes about your personality? The styles and fabrics you are drawn to can determine your clothing character. Your favorite outfits hold the clues. Consider what you like to wear, then compare it with the descriptions below to piece together your personality style.

- My favorite bottoms are...
    - a. trendy studded denims
    - b. perfectly pressed khakis
    - c. durable trousers
    - d. sweatpants

- My style can best be described as...
    - a. fun and flashy
    - b. tailored and timeless
    - c. active and authoritative
    - d. casual and comfy

- I like fabrics that are...
    - a. modish
    - b. wrinkle-free
    - c. dependable
    - d. relaxed

- I like colors that are...
    - a. flamboyant
    - b. neutral
    - c. bold
    - d. monotone

- My favorite shoes are...
    - a. showy stilettos
    - b. polished pumps
    - c. functional flats
    - d. snug sneakers

Now, match your picks to your personality!

- **A—stylin' sanguine:** You love to talk, tell stories, and have fun! Your voice, body gestures, and clothing are all loud and dramatic.

- **B—meticulous melancholy:** You like things perfect, organized, and structured. Your voice, body gestures, and wardrobe are all subtle.

- **C—chic choleric:** You're a natural-born leader who demands respect and attention. Your voice, body gestures, and clothes are powerful.

- **D—relaxed-fit phlegmatic:** You're basically easygoing and peaceful by nature. Your voice, body gestures, and attire are all low-key.

MakeOver Minute #60
OVEREXTENDED

Do you ever find yourself overextended? Are your time and resources depleted? Do you meet yourself coming and going, trying to get ahead but finding yourself further behind? Well, paying your bills on time is a testament of your love and obedience to God.

I once heard a story about a gal who was overextended and could not pay all her bills at one time. She would place them in a bowl and draw them out one by one, writing a check for each in the order in which she drew it, until the money was gone. One month, a creditor she had neglected to pay phoned to demand payment. The gal responded, "If you don't leave me alone, I won't even put you in the bowl!" Now, no matter how silly that may sound, how many people find themselves with too few dollars when the monthly bills arrive?

Pay your debt as it comes due. Neglecting your bills is a sin. If you simply cannot pay for whatever reason, call those you owe, explain your situation, and ask for a reduction in payment or a new payment schedule. Most creditors would rather you pay something than nothing at all.

As a Christian, God expects you to be a good steward with what you've been given.

It's all about what we do with what we have—investing in someone instead of something. Don't squander your time and money on things you don't need, but spend them on others as an example of what Christ did for you.

> *Pay your debts as they come due. However, one debt you can never finish paying is the debt of love that you owe each other.*

—Romans 13:8 GOD'S WORD

Prayer and Praise / Thankful Thoughts: _____

_____

_____

_____

Hair and eyelash extensions have become wildly popular over the past few years, and it's easy to see why. They give you the long, lush styles you want without the wait. Let's take a look at some of the most popular options so you can decide whether hair or lash extensions are right for you.

- **Custom-made, clip-on hair extensions** are some of the most natural-looking and healthiest for the hair. A stylist orders human hair close to your type and colors it to match your own hair. He or she then applies it by attaching the tiny clip-on combs so they will stay put. The downside is that the extensions are only designed for daily use and should not be slept in. They are, however, reusable, and with some practice you can learn to apply them yourself.

- **Fused or bonded extensions**, according to expert Rachel Quinn, are pieces or strands of hair that are fused to your own natural hair shaft to give it fullness, body, curl, or color. This type of extension must be applied by a professional, and the process takes anywhere from two to six hours. These extensions will last from two weeks to six months, depending on the gluing process. Hair extensions are a fun way to quadruple your hair's volume and lengthen it instantaneously, but they can be difficult to sleep on until you get used to them.

- **Synthetic add-ons** are the least expensive of all hair extensions and can be purchased at most beauty supply stores. They come in a variety of colors and styles—everything from clip-on to headband to scrunchy to pull-through types. The drawback is that synthetic add-ons have a short lifespan because they frizz easily. To make them last longer, don't wear them every day. Instead, save them for when you need a boost of confidence or for those special occasions.

- **Eyelash extensions**, like bonded hair extensions, are professionally applied to your own individual lashes and last between two and three months. The initial treatment is rather pricey, and touch-ups are not much less. The perks of eyelash extensions include achieving length and thickness without the mess of mascara.

- **False eyelashes** are an inexpensive alternative to extensions. They add volume and length without breaking the bank. Two types are available—strip lashes that are glued across the base of your lash line and single lashes that are applied where needed.

MakeOver Minute #61
SPECIAL VALUE

Make the most of what you've been given. For years, I didn't grasp this concept. I reasoned that if I bought something at a super-duper clearance sale, I could probably find a use for it no matter what it was. Once I bought a pair of snowshoes that were marked down 90 percent. *Wow, what a savings!* I thought as I rushed to the register to pay for my find. Now mind you, I lived in Virginia Beach, Virginia, at the time, where I would never have a need for snowshoes. I rationalized the purchase by assuming that since my husband was in the navy, we might get transferred to an area where we would need snowshoes. Well, gals, that was more than 16 years ago, and I have yet to need snowshoes even once!

If you buy something you never wear, it has zero value, even if you bought it at a special discounted price. This, dear friends, is a waste of time and money.

I do want to point out, friends, that time is of the essence. There is no time to waste, so don't complicate your lives unnecessarily. Keep it simple...Even in ordinary things—your daily routines of shopping, and so on.
—1 Corinthians 7:29-30

You are accountable to God for what you have and for what you do with what you've been given. Use your resources wisely. Shop shrewd, save smart, and serve sincerely. Love God with all you've got.

Honor GOD with everything you own; give him the first and the best.
—Proverbs 3:9

Prayer and Praise / Thankful Thoughts: _____

_____

_____

_____

Have you ever thought about what you could do with all the money you've wasted on clothes you've never worn? I'm sure I could have taken a world cruise, bought a new car, or saved a nice chunk of change for retirement by now. We all waste money on clothes that never see the light of day. They hang in the back of the closet—sometimes with the tags still on them—until we eventually get rid of them.

We end up with clothes we don't wear because we tend to shop without boundaries. We buy things without a plan or just because they're on sale, and this kind of senseless shopping wreaks havoc on the budget. Smart shopping starts by keeping you and your needs in mind. It's okay to shop the clearance racks, but don't buy something just because it's cheap. Only buy what brings value to your wardrobe.

- **Shop for your shape.** Are you a triangle, wedge, rectangle, figure eight, or circle? A triangle shape is smaller on the top than the bottom. A wedge is just the opposite—wider shoulders, narrower hips and waist. A rectangle is straight up and down, while a figure eight is curvaceous and a circle is round. The correct shape of garment will move with your body and flatter your figure instead of working against it.

- **Collect your color.** Choose colors that enhance your skin tone. Certain colors make you look healthier and more radiant, with or without makeup. (See MakeOver Minute #19 for details.)

- **Clean the closet.** Make a clean sweep of your closet. Get rid of anything that doesn't fit or isn't the right color. Integrate the keepers into your wardrobe, and fill in with additional wardrobe pieces if necessary. For example, if you have a great suit that needs a new blouse, buy one or two tops to match that particular suit. Also, update what you have on hand with inexpensive but trendy accessories.

- **Save for sales.** Waiting for a sale is a great way to stretch your wardrobe dollars. Most retail stores discount fall and winter items in January or February, and spring and summer clothes in June or July. Another way to make the most of your money is to shop discount, vintage, thrift, consignment, outlet stores, or to shop E-Bay. If time is a consideration, shop online, but be sure to calculate shipping charges and read the return policy before you click on the checkout button.

Get the look you want for less by shopping smarter. Cash in on clothing sense, and plan now what to do with all the money you'll save.

MakeOver Minute #62
IT'S IN THE BAG

When I was just a little girl, probably only five or six years old, my auntie taught me a valuable lesson. It was just before Easter when she presented me with a shiny new patent leather pocketbook, complete with two newly polished pennies inside. I asked her why she put the pennies in my purse, and she shared with me this passage of Scripture:

> *As Jesus sat facing the temple offering box, he watched how [much] money people put into it. Many rich people put in large amounts. A poor widow dropped in two small coins, worth less than a cent. He called his disciples and said to them, "I can guarantee this truth: This poor widow has given more than all the others."*
>
> —Mark 12:41-43 GOD'S WORD

From what the Scripture says, I can imagine the wealthy, giving openly and wanting all to see their generosity. Then I picture this woman—hungry, dressed in rags, in desperate need herself—reaching into her pocket and searching for something to give. Just then, Jesus tells His disciples to sit up and pay attention. The disciples watch the woman as she rifles through her pocket, pulls out two coins, and drops them in the box. I'm sure the disciples were thinking, *What's the big deal? She didn't give anything of value.* Jesus, knowing their thoughts, refutes them, saying, "Yes, she did—she gave her all."

The poor woman didn't have much to give, but in God's eyes she could not have given any more. The value of the gift was not determined by its amount, but by the spirit in which it was given. She gave with an attitude of generosity and gratitude.

What's in your bag? Do you give grudgingly or graciously? If Jesus was watching you—and He is—what would you give, and how would you give it? My auntie taught me that even two cents can be a huge amount when you're giving your all.

> *All these others made offerings that they'll never miss; she gave extravagantly what she couldn't afford—she gave her all!*
>
> —Luke 21:4

At first thought, your purse may seem like nothing more than something you carry your stuff around in. But in reality, the type of handbag you choose carries a lot of weight. The wrong size, style, or shape can make or break the look you're going for. After all, your purse projects your image. You want one that works *for* you as well as *with* you.

Picking a purse that's the right size is the most important thing to consider as you shop for a handbag. One that is too big or too small can add or detract from your body image. Always make sure you try on a purse for size before you buy it. Like clothes, you want one that fits.

Use the tips below to help you pick the perfect purse proportioned to your size and stature. If you're in the market for a special occasion bag, choose a small and dainty purse that will complement your outfit.

- **Petite gals,** more than any others, need to consider purse size. Smaller frames need smaller pocketbooks. Choose one that matches your size and shape, avoiding large bags that will overshadow you. If you are not sure where to begin, try a small clutch or satchel design.

- **Tall girls** should stick with a medium to oversize bag. A small bag with a short strap will make you look taller and will look proportionately off-balance. Instead, try a sling style on for size.

- **Plus sizes** do well with a hobo-style bag. Stay away from small purses that will make you look larger than you really are.

- **Top-heavy women** who appear slim from the hips down but have a tummy should sport a larger-style messenger bag with a long strap.

- **Bottom-heavy gals** will bring balance to their shape by carrying a shoulder bag that fits snugly under the arm, visually drawing the eye to the upper body.

- **Hourglass figures** can accentuate their shape with a medium-sized shoulder bag that hangs down to the waist.

MakeOver Minute #63
TIMES ARE CHANGIN'

When I was in my teens, the television show *Three's Company* debuted. It was quite controversial at the time. The show was based on two girls and one guy living together in a platonic relationship. The mere thought of the two sexes rooming together outside of marriage was definitely not accepted in mainstream America. Now, not only have we consented to coed, but we've also accepted couples living together and sleeping in the same bed. Many have altered their thinking regarding this issue, but has God?

The ways of the world are constantly changing, and if we as believers shift our thinking to agree with what goes against Scripture, we will fall. Build your house—the temple of God—on His Word, and you will stand firm even in the shiftiest of circumstances.

Anyone who listens to my teaching and obeys me is wise, like a person who builds a house on solid rock. Though the rain comes in torrents and the floodwaters rise and the winds beat against that house, it won't collapse, because it is built on rock. But anyone who hears my teaching and ignores it is foolish, like a person who builds a house on sand. When the rains and floods come and the winds beat against that house, it will fall with a mighty crash.

—Matthew 7:24-27 NLT

Where do you stand? Is your house built on the Rock? It isn't God who moves away—it's you who distance yourself from Him. Faithfulness to God is key to living fulfilled at any age. It doesn't matter to God if you are in your teens, 20s, 30s, or beyond. His expectations are the same—obedience to Him at all ages. Build your beliefs on Him, and you will remain solid even when things shift.

God is our constant. Even in this ever-changing world, we can trust our unchanging Lord.

Jesus Christ is the same yesterday, today, and forever.

—Hebrews 13:8 NKJV

When I was in my teens, I thought I knew it all, and my greatest challenge was graduating from high school. In my 20s, I had something to prove, and my chief anxiety was overcoming my fear to try. In my 30s, I believed I could do it all, and my main concern was keeping up appearances.

My, how things change! Now that I'm in my 40s, I realize three things. First—how little I know. Second—living a performance-based life is futile. Third—setting limitations is a sign of maturity, not disability. I don't know what my 50s, 60s, and 70s hold, but I know one thing—I'll relish my 80s, when I can speak my mind without offending anyone. They'll just assume senility has set in!

Our lives are changing, and hopefully for the better. It's not that they're getting any easier. It's just that age, for the most part, offers a better understanding of life. And although we're growing up on the inside, there's no reason to mature at the same pace on the outside. It's okay to look in the mirror and see yourself as the best you've ever been, no matter if you're twentysomething, thirtysomething, fortysomething, or beyond. Here's how you can look your best at *any* age.

1. **Practice proper skin care**. No matter your age or skin type, it's always important to take care of your face. The minute you start to clean, pamper, nourish, and protect your skin, you'll begin to reap the benefits. Find a skin-care system that is specially formulated for your skin type.

2. **Update your hairdo**. Don't get caught in a time warp with your hair. Try an updated new style, and remember—if you don't like it, it will grow out. Find a style or two you like in a current magazine, and take the pictures with you to the hairdresser. Ask the stylist if either will work for your hair type, and how difficult the styles will be for you to do at home. If what you chose won't work, ask the stylist for recommendations.

3. **Flair up your fashion.** Dowdy is out, and updated is in. You don't have to dress like a teenager, but a few youthful accessories never hurt anybody. Spice up your wardrobe with a fashionable belt, chic jewelry, or a trendy jacket.

MakeOver Minute #64
SEX APPEAL

Sex was designed by God as a gift to be shared between husband and wife. Sexual intimacy brings the two together to become one flesh for the purpose of procreation and pleasure. Yes, it's true—God delights in sex. He is the One who gave us our sexual drive and desire, and He created it to be a beautiful experience between man and wife. It's only when we turn it into something other than what God designed it to be that it becomes dirty, disgusting, and destructive. Here's what Jesus said when the Pharisees questioned him one time:

> He answered, "Haven't you read in your Bible that the Creator originally made man and woman for each other, male and female? And because of this, a man leaves father and mother and is firmly bonded to his wife, becoming one flesh—no longer two bodies but one. Because God created this organic union of the two sexes, no one should desecrate his art by cutting them apart."
>
> —Matthew 19:4-6

Past hurts, abuse, or a difficult upbringing can often distort a woman's view of sex. In these cases, help and healing are necessary to bring a wife out of her inhibitions and into sexual fulfillment. Meeting each other's needs is not only ordained by God, but necessary in order to avoid sexual temptation.

> Because there is so much sexual immorality, each man should have his own wife, and each woman should have her own husband. The husband should not deprive his wife of sexual intimacy, which is her right as a married woman, nor should the wife deprive her husband. The wife gives authority over her body to her husband, and the husband also gives authority over his body to his wife. So do not deprive each other of sexual relations. The only exception to this rule would be the agreement of both husband and wife to refrain from sexual intimacy for a limited time, so they can give themselves more completely to prayer. Afterward they should come together again so that

Satan won't be able to tempt them because of their lack of self-control.

—1 Corinthians 7:2-5 NLT

Celebrate your marriage just like you did on your wedding night. Plan, prepare, and please one another with the gift God reserved just for you and your husband.

GOD then used the rib that he had taken from the Man to make Woman and presented her to the Man. The Man said,

> *Finally! Bone of my bone,*
> *flesh of my flesh!*
> *Name her Woman*
> *for she was made from Man.*

Therefore a man leaves his father and mother and embraces his wife. They become one flesh...The two of them, the Man and his Wife, were naked, but they felt no shame.

—Genesis 2:22-25

I got up to open the door to my lover, sweetly ready to receive him, Desiring and expectant as I turned the door handle.

—Song of Solomon 5:5

I am my lover's, the one he desires.

—Song of Solomon 7:10 NLT

Prayer and Praise / Thankful Thoughts: _____

_____

_____

_____

Remember those days when you planned what you would wear and how you would look before the date? You paid attention to every detail, hoping he would notice too. You wanted everything just right for Mr. Right in order to win him over. He proposes, you accept—and you begin planning the wedding. You pick the perfect dress, shoes, and accessories, and—for your wedding night—you choose a pretty peignoir set sure to take his breath away. You look beautiful as you walk down the aisle, you say "I do," and that was the last time you did anything to make yourself look really good for your hubby.

Ladies, this is a huge pet peeve of mine! Women whine all the time about the lack of romance in their marriage, but when was the last time you made an effort to provoke it? It's a proven fact—men are visually stimulated. How you look plays a major role in your husband's response to you. Do you take time to make yourself pretty, or does your husband come home to you looking like an unmade bed?

I know what you're thinking: *But Tammy, I work all day, and the kids run me ragged. I barely have enough time to brush my teeth, let alone do my hair. Besides that I'm too worn out to play the role of the alluring lover.* Stop with the excuses! This attitude is not fair to you or your husband. Your marriage is a vital part of who you are, and when it becomes a low priority, you will suffer, grow apart, and even divorce if no effort is put forth.

Do yourself, your spouse, and marriage a favor by fixing yourself up. Before your hubby walks through the door this evening, spend some time primping. Style your hair, put on some makeup, change out of your sweats, and dab on some perfume. Greet him at the door with a kiss, and ask him about his day before you unload yours on him. He might be too shocked at first to respond, but trust me—he will.

Okay, so maybe your response to this is, "Tammy, I do all these things, and my marriage still lacks sizzle!" If that's the case, turn up the heat. If you're one of those gals who always takes care of herself and you still can't seem to get his attention, go the extra mile. Dare I tell you some of the things I've done to let my husband know he still lights my fire after all these years? I've picked him up from work wearing only a trench coat. I've kidnapped him for the weekend. I've staged many romantic dinners right here at home. Use your imagination and you'll discover that even on a budget, you can bring romance back to your marriage.

Turn up the sex appeal, make your husband a priority, and just like when you were dating, he'll take notice.

MakeOver Minute #65
THAT'S IT—PERIOD!

Enduring a period for three to four days once a month is bad enough, but can you imagine having a period that lasted for 12 years straight?

In Mark 5, we read about a woman who had suffered from hemorrhaging for 12 years. She had been treated by many doctors and had spent all her money, and she was still bleeding. Her period would not end. Moreover, back then a woman was considered unclean for the duration of her period, whether it was normal or not (see Leviticus 15:22-33). So for her to touch Jesus in her unclean state was a big deal. It can be thought of as either an act of desperation or a feat of faith.

In this case, I believe the woman's desperation is what drove her to act on her faith. Yet it is important to note that it is her faith that healed her. She believed in her heart that if only she could touch the hem of Jesus' garment, she would be cured. And it happened in just that way—the moment she touched Him, her bleeding stopped. She was made whole. She knew it, and Jesus knew it too. When the woman humbly revealed herself, Christ called her "daughter"—an endearing term that signified the healing of her body as well as the healing of her soul.

Friend, what are you suffering from—sickness, a broken relationship, unpleasant circumstances? Whatever it is, reach out to Jesus. He wants to bring hope and healing to the miserable periods of time in your life.

*He said to her, "Daughter, your faith
has healed you. Go in peace."*

—Luke 8:48 NIV

Prayer and Praise / Thankful Thoughts: _____

_____

_____

_____

That time of the month can be miserable! One moment you feel normal, then your period hits and you go from Dr. Jekyll to Mrs. Hyde—sometimes without warning. You get snappy, cranky, irritable, and tired. Everything annoys you to the point that you want to stay in bed, pull the covers over your head, and wake up when it's over. You're not alone. Eighty percent of women who are of childbearing age experience PMS symptoms of some type—most commonly headaches, cramping, bloating, fatigue, and food cravings. But there *are* some ways to effectively take the edge off your period.

- If you suffer from headaches or menstrual cramps, try over-the-counter medications such as Midol or Pamprin.

- Relieve cramping by taking a hot bubble bath. Light some candles, put in a CD, and relax.

- The hormonal changes that take place during your menstrual cycle affect you not only physically but also emotionally. Your period can cause erratic mood swings, which affect those around you. When you feel these moods coming on, do yourself and others a favor and take some alone time. Have a cup of hot tea and take a moment to chill out.

- Satisfy your cravings but don't overdo it. Nibble on a few M&Ms instead of a whole King Kong–size chocolate bar.

- Put in a chick flick, grab the popcorn, and work up a tear. Studies show that crying helps women to reduce stress.

- Go to bed early or sleep in late. Just 15 minutes more sleep can determine which side of the bed you wake up on.

- If you don't feel like cooking, order in. Once-a-month takeout can be deemed a special treat.

- If you're married, warn your husband when your period is about to arrive so he won't take your moodiness personally.

- Exercise helps you to destress and makes you feel better about yourself.

- Drink more water. Soda is loaded with sodium, which will only make you feel more bloated.

Most of all, remember that your period will not last forever, so get through it the best you can!

MakeOver Minute #66
STEP OUT IN CONFIDENCE

Self-esteem is based on your self-worth. Do you condemn or commend who you are? God does not want you to feel inferior—He's created you with purpose!

> *He saved us and called us to be his own people, not because of what we have done, but because of his own purpose and grace.*
>
> —2 Timothy 1:9 GNT

Gaining a healthy dose of confidence—not conceit, but God-fearing confidence—begins with faith. Believe that God can and will help you reach your maximum potential.

And be confident that God will strengthen and mature you until you meet Him face-to-face. He will never give up on you.

> *I am confident of this very thing, that He who began a good work in you will perfect it until the day of Christ Jesus.*
>
> —Philippians 1:6 NASB

Prayer and Praise / Thankful Thoughts: _____

_____

_____

_____

Have you ever thought about how much more you could accomplish if you just had the confidence to try? A healthy amount of self-esteem is what allows you to take risks, speak up, and do things outside the norm.

Did you ever want to be a cheerleader but didn't have the nerve to try? Or did you want that promotion but were too afraid to ask? So many of life's opportunities pass us by because we're too self-conscious to act. We spend our time wishing we'd said or done something different and dreaming about how things might have been. Well, it's time to start working at building up your confidence level. Get ready to turn self-consciousness into self-confidence by practicing the following steps.

1. **Be optimistic.** Think and speak positively. Be an encourager rather than a discourager. People will value this about you, which will add to your own feelings of self-worth.

2. **Don't put yourself down.** Depreciating yourself annoys others and drives them away instead of attracting them to you.

3. **When you look in the mirror, focus on your best attributes.** Avoid nitpicking yourself to death. Accentuating the positive automatically downplays the negative.

4. **Journal your accomplishments.** Write down the good stuff, remembering there are glimmers of hope even in poor circumstances. I once talked to a gal who had recently lost her job and was in desperate need of money, but still was able to enjoy the blessing of being helped by others. Her achievement in this case was humility.

5. **Speak up.** This can be one of the most difficult things to do. In fact, did you know the number-one fear of most people is public speaking? We don't like to say anything even though we want to be heard! The trick is knowing what you want to say and realizing that, once you get started, the words will come easier.

6. **Concentrate on the compliments instead of the criticisms.** Did you know that if you receive 99 favorable comments and 1 negative remark, it will be the one disparaging word you'll remember most? Change your focus. Unless you hear the same negative thing over and over again, choose to disregard it.

7. **Look your best.** It's a proven fact that when you look better, you feel better. And when you feel better, you're more confident in yourself.

Self-confidence won't happen overnight, but with a bit of effort you can boost your self-esteem a little at a time until you're no longer wondering what *could* have happened. Instead, you'll know with conviction what *did!*

MakeOver Minute #67
BORN TO SHOP

Did you know that you were born to shop? Yes, it's true! God created you to joyfully...

- **S**erve Him
- **H**onor Him
- **O**bey Him
- **P**raise Him

*Let every detail in your lives—words, actions, whatever—
be done in the name of the Master, Jesus, thanking God the
Father every step of the way.*

—Colossians 3:17

It's our daily mission to shop for opportunities to serve, honor, obey, and praise God throughout our lives. Everything we say and do should glorify Him and Him alone.

- **Serve Him:** "Serve only the LORD your God and fear him alone. Obey his commands, listen to his voice, and cling to him" (Deuteronomy 13:4 NLT). Serve God by serving others. Share a meal, babysit, run errands, and seek out other creative ways to administer God's grace to others.

- **Honor Him:** "All honor to the God and Father of our Lord Jesus Christ, for it is by his boundless mercy that God has given us the privilege of being born again. Now we live with a wonderful expectation because Jesus Christ rose again from the dead" (1 Peter 1:3 NLT). Honor God for who He is, and for who He allowed you to be through Christ.

- **Obey Him:** "Those who obey God's word really do love him. That is the way to know whether or not we live in him" (1 John 2:5 NLT). Obey God. Obedience to Him is the sincerest expression of love.

- **Praise Him:** "All praise to the God and Father of our Lord Jesus Christ. He is the source of every mercy and the God who comforts us"

(2 Corinthians 1:3 NLT). Praise God for His greatness and goodness in all situations and all circumstances.

You were born to **SHOP**—serve, honor, obey, and praise God for His benefit. Service gives honor, and obedience brings praise to God.

I have God's more-than-enough, more joy in one ordinary day than they get in all their shopping sprees.

—Psalm 4:6-7

Prayer and Praise / Thankful Thoughts: _____

_____

_____

_____

I have often thought that if shopping were an Olympic event, I'd be a strong contender for the gold medal! For me, shopping is more of a sport than a leisurely activity. It's the thrill of the hunt and the triumphant victory of finding the highest quality at the lowest price. It's all about knowing where to shop and how to shop to your benefit. Various shopping venues have their advantages and disadvantages, and knowing them is key to shopping like a pro.

- **Auctions:** My favorite shopping experience is an auction, where I'm in control of what I spend. Before you bid, keep a few things in mind:

  1. Before you travel a great distance, find out what's for sale and whether or not the auction is open to the public.

  2. Thoroughly inspect the item you're interested in before the bidding starts. If the item is damaged, what will it take and how much will it cost to restore it?

  3. Set a price limit before you bid so you don't get carried away and spend more than the item is worth. As you determine the price, don't forget to add in the tax and the buyer's premium if there is one.

4. Listen carefully for bidding instructions. Sometimes there are quantity minimums.

5. If you bid on something without meaning to, let the auctioneer know immediately.

- **Yard sales, flea markets, and thrift shops:** One woman's junk is another woman's treasure! Rummaging at these spots can lead to fabulous finds at just the right price.

   1. To save time, map out your rummage route in advance.

   2. Wear comfy shoes.

   3. Bring plenty of cash (in small bills), a checkbook, and proper ID with you.

   4. Arrive early for the best finds.

   5. Keep in mind that items are sold "as is" with a no-return policy.

   6. When appropriate, be prepared to barter. Ask, "What's your best price?" then counter it by saying, "Would you take x-amount in cash right now?"

   7. Bring along your own packing supplies, such as bags, blankets, or bubble wrap.

- **Shopping at home:** Catalogs, home-shopping networks, and the Internet can be a relaxing alternative to getting out and pounding the pavement. However, like other forms of shopping, you need to keep some things in mind.

   1. Know with whom you are dealing. Is this a reputable operation?

   2. What guarantees does the company have, and what is their return policy? Always read the fine print.

   3. What are the shipping and handling fees?

   4. Protect your privacy. Only order from a secure server online.

   5. Check the delivery date.

- **Department, discount, and specialty stores:** Department stores can save you time and money when you plan your schedule around sales events. When you have time to roam, discount stores can be a great place to find deals. And while specialty shops might cost you a little more, they can save you time if they're tailored to your tastes.

1. Avoid impulse buys. Whenever possible, plan your spending around sales. Ask for a rain check if the item you want is sold out.

2. Watch for unadvertised specials.

3. To save more, buy at the end of a season.

4. Beware of fancy packaging that will cost you more.

5. Know the store's return policy, and use it when a purchase does not meet your expectations.

MakeOver Minute #68
HOT FLASH

Menopause is the natural process of a woman's menstrual cycle ceasing and her childbearing years coming to an end. Although it is often associated with hormonal, physical, and psychological changes, menopause is not the end of your youthfulness or your sexuality.

God never meant for your worth to be judged by age or fluctuating hormone levels. He has a purpose and plan for your life, no matter your physical changes or challenges. God made it clear in His Word that there is a time for everything, which includes "the change."

Think of two postmenopausal women who were instrumental in the lineage and events surrounding the birth of Jesus Christ. *Sarah* was "mother of the nations." She remained childless until she was 90 years old, at which time God told her she would bear a son and name him Isaac. God promised to establish an everlasting covenant with Isaac and all of his descendants, which included the lineage of Christ (see Genesis 17:15-19).

Elizabeth was a mentor to Mary, the mother of Jesus. In Elizabeth's old age, she finally conceived a child, John the Baptist, who was the faithful forerunner to the Messiah (see Luke chapter 1).

So you see, there *is* life after menopause! Remember, God can use you at any age and at any stage, as long as you remain faithful to Him.

I know that there is nothing better for them than to be happy and enjoy themselves as long as they live.
—Ecclesiastes 3:12 NRS

Prayer and Praise / Thankful Thoughts: _____

_____

_____

_____

Whether it affects you directly or indirectly, menopause can be a miserable time of life for all of those involved. Going through "the change" can be agonizing for both you and your loved ones. I remember all too well my mother's menopausal days and the extreme mood swings that kept our family on edge. We understood she was physically tormented, and we also knew her irrational moods were symptoms of her condition. As hard as it was, we had to learn to separate the illness from the individual in order to cope.

Make no mistake—menopause can be brutal. I know, because I've now entered the premenopausal state. I experience hot flashes and night sweats, which has prompted me to explore ways to make menopause more manageable for me and more bearable for my family. I've gleaned the following advice from women who have been or are going through menopause and wish to make it easier for the rest of us.

"Try to stay positive, and remember—it won't last forever" (Betty).

"Wear layers of clothing so that when the hot flashes hit, you can strip down without exposing yourself" (Sue).

"If you have night sweats, try hot-flash pajamas and sheet sets. They absorb the moisture so you don't wake up drenched" (JoAnne).

"I know you don't want to hear it, but a healthy diet and exercise really do help relieve menopausal stress" (Pat).

"Birth control is still necessary during menopause. Trust me—I know!" (Patty).

"Get support. Talk to a trusted friend or family member who can understand what's going on. Their love and encouragement is invaluable through the rough spots" (Judy).

"Limit your caffeine intake so that you can sleep better" (Beth).

"If you notice a decline in your sex drive, try an over-the-counter hormone supplement" (Margo).

"I am normally a very upbeat person. However, when menopause hit, so did depression. My doctor prescribed an antidepressant that really helped me survive the change" (Karen).

The good news about menopause is—like puberty—*this too shall pass.*

MakeOver Minute #69
BREAKING BREAD

The Last Supper, as it is known, was the final Passover meal Jesus shared with His disciples before His crucifixion (see Luke 22:14-20). Today, we continue to celebrate the Lord's Supper at the communion table. This is a time when believers break bread and drink from the cup to remember Christ—as well as what He did for us and why He did it.

And the proper table etiquette, if you will, is based on manners that reflect brokenness—Jesus' brokenness for us and our ongoing brokenness before Him. God cares about the heart of the matter.

> *The sacrifice you want is a broken spirit. A broken and repentant heart, O God, you will not despise.*
>
> —Psalm 51:17 NLT

Prayer and Praise / Thankful Thoughts: _____

_____

_____

_____

When I was growing up, my family had a rule that no matter what your daily schedule consisted of, you had to be home for the family supper. Little did I realize then how much I learned at the family table. This was an opportune time for me to learn everything from setting a table to basic table manners.

Things have changed a great deal since then. These days, many families do not sit down to meals together except on special occasions—and it shows! Many businesses across the nation are discovering that prospective job candidates lack basic social skills that were once taught in their youth.

Mom, it's time to ring the dinner bell and call your family to the table. Let's get back to the basics and teach the next generation good manners at home so they won't be socially inept when they go out in public.

- Always say *please* and *thank you* to your server as well as to your host.

- As soon as you sit down at the table, put your napkin in your lap.

- Take time to say grace.

- Always pass food to the right.

- Do not reach across the table. Instead, ask for the food to be passed to you.

- Sit up straight, keep your elbows off the table, and never talk with food in your mouth.

- Choose pleasant topics that make for polite conversation. Never use the dinner table as a place to scold.

- Take small bites. Never chew with your mouth open, and do not chomp.

- The polite way to eat soup is to spoon it away from you.

- Start with the dinner utensils on the outside and work your way in. Your salad fork is on the far left, and your main entree fork is the one next to it. Your soup spoon is on the far right, next to your teaspoon and knife. Your dessert spoon and fork are placed above your plate.

- Drink glasses are placed to your right, and your bread plate is on your left.

- Break your dinner roll into small pieces and eat it one piece at a time.

- If you need to leave the table, say, "Excuse me, please," and place your napkin on your seat or on the arm of your chair.

- Do not blow your nose or play with your hair at the table.

- When you're finished, place your eating utensils at the four o'clock position across your plate.

Whether you're at home or out on the town, manners truly matter!

MakeOver Minute #70
CRAZED FADS

Religious fads are all the rage. Developed by man, cults are based on an element of truth, which gives them just enough credibility to sound legit. For the most part, the group's leader testifies of profound revelation through either a vision or some other type of spiritual divination.

I am shocked that you are turning away so soon from God, who in his love and mercy called you to share the eternal life he gives through Christ. You are already following a different way that pretends to be the Good News but is not the Good News at all. You are being fooled by those who twist and change the truth concerning Christ.

—Galatians 1:6-7 NLT

Cults tend to gather followers with what appear to be generous expressions of care and concern. They prey on the depressed, the dejected, and the downtrodden, luring them in by offering to meet their deepest needs. They seem to be sound, but beneath the surface they're specious.

Know what you believe and why you believe it. Operate off fact rather than feeling. Base your faith on the truth of the Word of God, and know it well enough so that if you encounter twisted teachings, you won't be fooled into accepting a faddish fake rather than the real thing.

I want you also to be smart, making sure every "good" thing is the real thing. Don't be gullible in regard to smooth-talking evil.

—Romans 16:19

Prayer and Praise / Thankful Thoughts: _____

_____

_____

_____

Do you remember poodle skirts, mood rings, pet rocks, jelly shoes, or Beanie Babies? These are all blasts from the past—fads from years gone by. These were must-haves from the '50s, '60s, '70s, '80s, and '90s—things we said were hip, up-to-the-minute, fab, and fabulous! The question is, where are these items now? Unless you're a pack rat, chances are you threw them out long ago.

The latest fashion trends and crazes keep us always wanting more. Every season, we shop for what's "in" so we can be faddishly in style. We want to be in vogue, but this can come at a price. Think back to the first time you saw a particular fashion fad. Did you like it immediately, or did it have to grow on you? I remember the fingerless lace gloves that were popular in the '80s. I didn't really like them and they weren't very comfortable, yet I *had* to have them because everyone else was wearing them. I think I wore my pair once—maybe twice—and that was it. Those gloves were definitely not worth the money, but they did teach me a valuable lesson—if you've gotta get a must-have fad, buy it cheap. It's not wrong to indulge a fad fetish, but don't spend a lot doing it.

Splurge on the basics, then add a few inexpensive, trendy pieces. For example, buy a quality pair of basic black pants, then top them off with a cheap modern belt. Or purchase a classy jacket and wear it with a low-cost trendy top.

Most fads last two seasons at best, so shop discount stores for knockoffs in order to avoid designer prices. When the item goes out of style, you won't feel guilty about getting rid of it.

Dressing stylishly doesn't mean you have to wear what's current. Fashion repeats itself. Try shopping vintage stores or E-Bay for the latest looks for less. A couple years ago, brooches were all the rage. They were quite pricey at the malls, so I searched antique stores for the best buys. I found gorgeous resale pins at a fraction of the retail price.

Fads sizzle, but they also fizzle out. One day they're hot, the next they're not. So don't invest too much money in something that won't pay off. Just realize that today's must-haves will be tomorrow's has-beens.

MakeOver Minute #71
MAKE A SPECTACLE OF YOURSELF

Even the boldest of the bold can be manipulated by peer pressure. Take Peter, for example. He was bold enough to walk on water with Christ (see Matthew 14:22-33), yet he denied his Lord three times (see Mark 14:66-72). We know Peter's heart in this situation, because Scripture tells us that he broke down and wept when he realized his failure.

I don't know about you, but I'm like Peter in so many ways. I want to be bold and speak up and out for Christ, but sometimes I don't, and this makes my heart sad. Just the other day on an airplane flight, the gentleman next to me slandered the church on the topic of homosexuality. I sat there intimidated for a moment, then boldly spoke up: "Be careful what you say, because I'm part of the church." He looked at me in surprise, then politely apologized and changed the subject. It's not that I said anything profound—it's just that I stood my ground and, I hope, gave him something to think about in the process.

Don't allow people to intimidate you. Stand up for what you believe and make a spectacle of yourself in and through the Spirit of God.

God doesn't want us to be shy with his gifts,
but bold and loving and sensible.

—2 Timothy 1:7

We have become a spectacle to the entire world—
to people and angels alike.

—1 Corinthians 4:9b NLT

Prayer and Praise / Thankful Thoughts: _____

_____

_____

_____

How many times have you tried on numerous pairs of sunglasses, only to leave the store discouraged because nothing looked right or felt good?

Finding the right style and color of frames for your face shape and skin tone can be a daunting task when you don't know what to look for. Let's take a look at what you've been missing so you can narrow down the selection and have success with your spectacles.

For the perfect frames, factor in two things—the color of your skin and the shape of your face. Do you have a warm skin tone with yellow or gold undertones, or is your skin tone cool with blue or pink undertones?

Warm frame colors include gold, khaki, tortoise, copper, orange, coral, off-white, orange-red, warm violet, yellow-green, and brown. Cool frame colors include silver, white, black, blue, blue-red, plum, magenta, pink, purple, blue-green, and gray.

The shape of your frames should complement the size and shape of your face. The frame size should match the scale of your face size, and the shape of the frame should bring balance to it. Which shape are you?

- **Round:** Make a round face appear thinner and longer by trying narrow, rectangular frames that are wider than they are deep.

- **Oval:** To visually keep the oval shape's natural balance, look for glasses that are proportionately to scale with the size of your face. Choose glasses that are as wide as the broadest part of your face, and not too deep or too narrow.

- **Oblong:** To visually minimize the length and bring balance, try frames that cover as much of the center of the face as possible.

- **Square:** To make a square face look longer and soften the angles, choose a slender frame that has more width than depth, such as narrow ovals.

- **Heart:** To balance the top of the face with the bottom, try frames with vertical lines and a thin-rimmed—or rimless—style.

- **Triangle:** Add width to the upper part of your face by wearing glasses that are detailed on the top half, like cat-eye shapes.

MakeOver Minute #72
DRESS FOR SUCCESS

Dressing for success is not only about the clothes you put on your body—it also has to do with the way you outfit your mind. Scripture tells us that the struggles we face are not against flesh and blood, even though they may take on that appearance, like in the case of a wayward teen. In reality, what you're dealing with is Satan and his evil forces. He's the one who is desperately trying to make you look bad and feel like a failure.

Put on all the armor that God gives you, so that you will be able to stand up against the Devil's evil tricks. For we are not fighting against human beings but against the wicked spiritual forces in the heavenly world, the rulers, authorities, and cosmic powers of this dark age. So put on God's armor now! Then when the evil day comes, you will be able to resist the enemy's attacks; and after fighting to the end, you will still hold your ground.

—Ephesians 6:11-13 GNT

Satan doesn't want you dressed and ready to move forward in the armor of God. Instead, he's hoping you'll take a more casual approach and dress down so he can attack when your defenses are weak. The enemy targets vulnerability.

Be careful! Watch out for attacks from the Devil, your great enemy. He prowls around like a roaring lion, looking for some victim to devour.

—1 Peter 5:8 NLT

Dress for success in the full armor of God, and you will be the victor rather than the devil's victim.

- Strap on the **belt of truth**. God's absolute truth will shed light on Satan's lies.

- Safeguard yourself with the **righteousness of God**. Know you are secure in Christ, not because of anything you did, but because of what Jesus did on your behalf.

- Secure your feet in the **gospel of peace,** so that you're always ready to share God's love anytime and anywhere.

- Take up the **shield of faith**. Exercise it, nurture it, and live it.

- Shelter your mind with the **knowledge of salvation**. If you don't take control of your thinking, the enemy will.

- Strike with the **sword of the Spirit**. Quote Scripture, and the devil will flee.

So put on God's armor now! Then when the evil day comes,
you will be able to resist the enemy's attacks.

—Ephesians 6:13 GNT

Prayer and Praise / Thankful Thoughts: _____

_____

_____

_____

Dressing for success means dressing for the job you want, not for the one you have. If you want to be a manager, dress like the managers do—unless, of course, your job requires you to wear a uniform. In that situation, it's all about adopting the attitude of the position you want instead of the attire.

When it comes to your workplace wardrobe, you want to look your professional best yet also fit in with the company's official—or unofficial—dress code. You want to project the same image as your boss, or your boss's boss. But be careful not to overdo it, because looking *too* good can provoke feelings of jealousy, especially among other women.

In today's society, dressing for success takes on a whole new meaning. Times have changed, and so has business attire. We've gone from neat and tidy to casual and sloppy. In fact, many companies have adopted "casual Fridays," a day when dressing down is condoned. However, let me share an e-mail I received about this very subject. It's from a college graduate who came to me for advice on how to dress for a job interview.

Dear Tammy,

I followed your wardrobe advice and got the first job I interviewed for. Not only that, I applied everything else you said about dressing for the job I ultimately want, and guess what? While everyone else was dressing down on Friday, which is a casual day, I didn't, and that got me noticed. My boss actually said, "You are getting this promotion because you always project a professional image." Thanks to you, in less than a year's time I am getting noticed and already moving up the ranks.

Thanks,
Callie

Let's take a look at the "career gear" basics I shared with Callie.

- High-quality shoes, a belt, a bag, or a briefcase—all in a matching color—are a must, but never carry a purse and a briefcase at the same time.

- When in doubt, dress conservatively.

- Makeup should appear polished and professional.

- Keep your hair neatly styled. Don't overdo it.

- Nails should be clean and neat and not too long.

- Invest in the best-quality basic black suit you can afford, and pull it together with a top that complements your skin tone.

- Prior to your interview, hang out in the company's parking lot or somewhere nearby the office to observe what other employees are wearing. Even if their attire looks casual, still dress it up a notch or two.

- Wear a nice, basic watch.

- Keep your shoes clean and polished.

- Buy a quality overcoat. These can often be found at resale shops.

- Keep undergarments under wraps. They shouldn't show at all.

- Don't overdo it with the perfume.

- Save hose with snags or runs to wear under trousers, never with a skirt.

- Carry baby wipes in case of spills.

- Clothes should always look neat, clean, and wrinkle-free.

- Buy a lint brush or roller, and use it!

MakeOver Minute #73
SWEAR BY HAIR

A trademark slogan of Clairol hair color states, "Hair color so natural only her hairdresser knows for sure." This means that your hair color will look so real, you can swear by it.

In Jesus' time, the Jews did just that—they would swear by their hair. In fact, in those days, making a vow by your head of hair had the same significance as putting your hand on the Bible and swearing by it.

Don't even swear, "By my head!" for you can't turn one hair white or black. Just say a simple, "Yes, I will," or "No, I won't." Your word is enough. To strengthen your promise with a vow shows that something is wrong.

—Matthew 5:36-37 NLT

In this passage of Scripture, Jesus emphasized the importance of keeping your word. People were breaking vows left and right, using sacred language to do it. They were making promises they couldn't or wouldn't keep.

What about you? What is your word worth? Would you stake your hair on it? Are you known for keeping your promises, or do they mean nothing? All too often, we get caught up in making empty promises that betray trust and destroy relationships. Don't swear by it if you don't intend to keep it. Be a woman of your word. Trust is the most important thing you have to offer.

A word out of your mouth may seem of no account, but it can accomplish nearly anything—or destroy it!

—James 3:5

Prayer and Praise / Thankful Thoughts: _____

_____

_____

_____

Just a hint of hair color can turn you from drab to fab in just a few minutes! The trick is in knowing the color and process that are right for you. First, choose a color that complements your natural skin tone. Then, decide if you're best off with a few highlights or all-over color. The other consideration is price—do you want to pay someone else to do it, or can you do it yourself? Let's find out the tricks of the trade that will help enlighten you on the process.

- **Color:** Pick a color that works with your complexion. If you have pink or blue undertones, opt for ash tints, which will neutralize your coloring. If you have sallow skin, choose a deep red or auburn. Stick with dark shades for an olive complexion.

- **Process:** Pick a process. Do you want all-over color or highlights? Keep in mind that all-over color needs to be touched up every three to five weeks, while highlights can last up to twelve weeks.

- **Place:** Do you want to visit a salon, or do you want to do the color yourself at home? Do-it-yourself hair color kits are great for busy people or those on a budget. With a few helpful reminders, you can become a pro at doing your own color.

  1. Rub petroleum jelly around your hairline and on your ears to avoid getting a dye line. If you do get dye on your skin, remove it with an alcohol-based toner.

  2. Always wear gloves, and drape an old towel around your shoulders.

  3. If you have long hair, buy two hair-color kits.

  4. If you've never colored your hair before, do a patch test at least 48 hours in advance to check for color and any allergic reaction.

  5. To get uniform coverage, start at the back of your head and work your way forward.

  6. Follow the directions that come with the color kit. In the event of a coloring mishap, call the company's telephone number printed on the back of the box before doing anything else.

After treatment, wait 48 hours to wash your hair. Always use shampoos and conditioners specially formulated for color-treated hair, which help your color last longer. Also, deep-condition your hair on a regular basis to keep it looking and feeling its best.

MakeOver Minute #74
SHOWERS OF BLESSINGS

Showers of blessing,
Showers of blessing we need.
Mercydrops round us are falling,
But for the showers we plead.

—Daniel W. Whittle

Do you know anyone who wouldn't want to be showered in blessings? I don't! Everyone I know is happy to receive blessings, but I do know of those who are stingy in sharing them. There are those who take, take, take—and those who give with all their heart.

I think of my great-aunt, who willingly helped others anytime she could. Once she helped someone out financially, even though she herself didn't have much money to spare. Later, that same person she'd helped came into a tidy sum of money, yet she never paid my great-aunt back. I told my great-aunt I thought it wasn't fair, but she told me not to hold a grudge against this person. Instead, I should put my energy into being a "blessin'" by praying for her.

> *Don't get tired of doing what is good. Don't get discouraged and give up, for we will reap a harvest of blessing at the appropriate time.*
>
> —Galatians 6:9 NLT

How can you be a blessing to someone? This isn't something you have to plan in advance or add to your Day-Timer, but you do have to be alert for opportunities. We should ask God to make us the blessing.

Make me a blessing; make me a blessing.
Out of my life may Jesus shine.
Make me a blessing, O Saviour, I pray.
Make me a blessing to someone today.

—Ira Wilson

> *Give away your life; you'll find life given back, but not merely given back—given back with bonus and blessing. Giving, not getting, is the way. Generosity begets generosity.*
>
> —Luke 6:38

_____

_____

_____

As much as I relish a hot bath, there's not always time for one. Most mornings, I'm in a rush to get out the door, so a shower has to be fast and efficient from start to finish. But did you know that you can turn even a ten-minute shower into a spa experience?

1. Close the bathroom door and turn on the water. While the water is heating, undress and apply a facial mask before you get in. The steam from the shower opens your pores so the mask can work below the skin's surface. And rinsing a mask off is easy in the shower!

2. Shampoo your hair twice—first with a clarifying shampoo to get rid of the gunk, then second with a shampoo formulated for your hair type.

3. Apply conditioner to your hair and let it work in while you shave your legs. Also, use hair conditioner instead of shaving gel, which saves you time and money while leaving your legs silky-smooth.

4. To make your shower seem less rushed and more relaxed, treat yourself to a lavender body bar or wash, which gently caresses your skin as it fills the shower with a heavenly aroma. Lavender has a calming effect to help you face your day feeling less stressed.

5. Keep your exfoliant in the shower. It's easier to thoroughly rinse the gritty exfoliant from your face while you're showering. To effectively exfoliate, put your face under warm (not hot) water and use circular motions to remove dead cells from the skin's surface.

6. When you get out of the shower, have two towels standing by—one for your hair and one for your body. Wring out your hair, then put it up in the towel. Next, briskly rub your body back and forth with a terry-cloth towel. This will stimulate blood flow, increase circulation, remove dead skin cells, and make your body glow.

7. I've saved the best tip for last—don't forget to sing! Start your day with a song. This is one place you can let your voice be heard, and you'll always sound good singing in the shower!

MakeOver Minute #75
FATTY ISSUES

As much as you hate the appearance of fatty, lumpy cellulite, have you ever wondered what it would be like if you could look in the mirror and see the effects of spiritual flab? Spiritual flab is caused by sin that deposits just enough spiritual fat to weigh us down and hold us back. Hebrews 12:1 in *The Message* paraphrase refers to these as "parasitic sins," which latch on and keep you from making any real progress in your spiritual growth. They make you feel just bad enough about yourself that you feel useless when it comes to serving God. We take on the attitude "I'm not good enough," yet God dispels that myth right at the beginning of the verse.

Since we are surrounded by so many examples [of faith],
we must get rid of everything that slows us down,
especially sin that distracts us. We must run the race that
lies ahead of us and never give up.

—Hebrews 12:1 GOD'S WORD

Many people in the Bible are incredible examples of faith. Moses was a murderer whom God used to lead His people out of Egypt. Then there was Rahab, the prostitute who delivered her family from destruction and was placed in the lineage of the Messiah. And of course we can't forget King David, the adulterer who penned the Psalms and, in his humility, became a man after God's own heart. Our role models are all imperfect people whom God used in spite of their sin. If God can use them, He can certainly use you!

So get rid of that unsightly sin that encumbers your relationship with God. To be effective, we must get into a routine of ridding ourselves of those sins that restrain us and remain dedicated to the race that is before us.

Do you see what this means—all these pioneers who blazed the
way, all these veterans cheering us on? It means we'd better
get on with it. Strip down, start running—and never quit!
No extra spiritual fat, no parasitic sins.

—Hebrews 12:1

_____

_____

_____

Cellulite is the term used to describe the fatty deposits under the skin that give it a lumpy appearance. As we gain weight, our fat cells swell while our connective tissue remains the same. Hormones, pregnancy, and the aging process all attribute to the weakening of the collagen fibers, causing this unsightly dimpling effect. Cellulite latches on to the majority of women, becoming an unsightly parasite on the hips, buttocks, and thighs. Bottom line—cellulite is fat. If you reduce the size of the fat cells, you can decrease the cottage-cheese appearance.

The best remedy for cellulite is diet and exercise. I'm sure you've heard it before, but allow me to say it again—drink plenty of water, avoid fatty foods, and work out at least five times a week. Unfortunately, outside of the hard work of diet and exercise, there's no surefire way to diminish cellulite, except with treatments performed by a dermatologist. You can, however, improve its appearance with these simple procedures.

- Topical cellulite creams or lotions are most effective when you massage them thoroughly into your skin, working in a circular motion with your fingertips.

- Massage the affected area with Epsom salts or sea salt while showering.

- Use a loofah when you bathe to stimulate circulation and break up fatty deposits.

- Take coffee grounds (regular, not decaf) that are still warm and massage them into the affected area. Next, wrap the area in plastic, being careful not to wrap it too tight and cut off your circulation. Leave it wrapped for 15 minutes, then remove and rinse.

In order to be effective, these techniques must be practiced on a regular basis. The key is dedication. You must establish a strict cellulite-reducing routine and stick with it.

MakeOver Minute #76
HANDIWORK

A few years ago, I met a gal who was a professional hand model. Her hands were absolutely, perfectly gorgeous. I asked her what she did to keep her hands looking so good, and she said she always wore sunblock, moisturized them religiously, and did nothing that might harm them. In fact, she had them insured—for a million dollars! Can you imagine your hands being worth so much?

When I was in the fifth grade, I learned the priceless value of hands. My friend Cindy's mother always wore gloves—even when gloves weren't fashionable. She had them in every color and in various lengths, and you never saw her without them. When I spent the night at Cindy's house, I finally saw her mother's hands without gloves. They looked terrible—splotchy, red, scarred, and quite disfigured. Later, when we were alone, I asked Cindy about them. She told me that when she was just a baby, their house caught fire. Her mother's hands were badly burnt in the process of saving Cindy's life. Beautiful to the eye they were not, but these were truly model hands.

Now let me tell you a story about another pair of model hands—hands that were nailed to a cross (see Matthew 27:35-44 and John 20:19-20). These hands were slammed, staked, and scarred on your behalf, and they offer the assurance of hope, help, and healing to the believer. These hands belong to our Lord and Savior, Jesus Christ. His priceless hands paid the price for your sins.

Beautiful hands come in many shapes and sizes and serve in many capacities. Some pick flowers for Mommy. Others do the dishes without being asked. Some bake bread for a neighbor, or serve in the front lines of our military. Beautiful hands are costly. Beautiful hands benefit others.

Let the beauty of the Lord our God be upon us, and establish the work of our hands for us; yes, establish the work of our hands.

—Psalm 90:17 NKJV

When we think about taking care of our aging skin, we usually don't think about our hands, even though the earliest signs of aging will often show up on them first. Our hands are exposed to water, cleaning chemicals, sun, cold, gardening, and endless amounts of work. As a result, they become dry, cracked, and sore. They end up looking and feeling old before their time.

Other people pay attention to your hands, but do you? The following tips will help you pamper your hands so they'll look smooth, feel soft, and keep your age a secret.

- At bedtime, **massage petroleum jelly into your hands** and put on a pair of cotton gloves. Your hands will soften as you sleep, and you'll wake up in the morning to subtly soft hands.

- **Get softer hands by exfoliating them** with a mixture of two tablespoons of olive oil, the juice of one lemon, and one-fourth cup organic sugar. Rub your hands together as if you're washing them, then rinse well. Follow up with your favorite hand moisturizer.

- **Wear gloves** to protect your hands when you're gardening, washing dishes, and cleaning with chemicals.

- Before you work in the garden, **scratch a bar of soap with your fingernails**. This will keep the dirt out and make your hands much easier to clean when you're finished working.

- **Apply lip balm** to cracked, peeling cuticles. This will soothe and somewhat protect them from the elements.

- **Treat yourself to a hand spa.** First, fill a bowl with warm water, then add a few drops of bubble bath. Next, apply cuticle oil to your cuticles and then soak your hands for five minutes. Then, exfoliate your hands to remove the dead skin cells. Finally, rinse your hands, towel dry, and apply moisturizer.

Your hands have a lot to do. Be good to them and they'll serve you well.

MakeOver Minute #77
TRADING SPACES

I'm a high-energy person by nature, so words like *rest*, *relax*, and *retreat* are rarely used in my vocabulary. However, I've learned that I need to apply them. We all need periods of rest—time to be still and let God be God.

My husband's temperament is the exact opposite of mine. When I'm rushed, he's relaxed; when I'm high-strung, he's low-key; and when I'm at my wit's end, he reminds me who is ultimately in control. His favorite line is, "Did God leave the throne?" I know this is my hint to stop stressing and start resting in the One who is ultimately in charge of the universe.

These are the times when I need to step back, find my place, and let God have His. At times like this, I retreat to my great-mom's rocker. It's my special place where I meet with God to bask in His love, refresh my mind through His Word, and pray over requests and ponder the responses. It's the place where I can be still and listen to God.

Make a date with God. Trade spaces for just a little while to meet Him in your own little corner of the world. Make it a priority to praise His Holy name (Psalm 138:2), read from His Holy Word (2 Timothy 3:15-17), and pray for holiness that you might be set apart to Him (1 Peter 1:16). Then sit quietly and listen for the whisper of God.

Be still, and know that I am God.

—Psalm 46:10 NKJV

Prayer and Praise / Thankful Thoughts: _____

_____

_____

_____

Do you have a beautiful space to call your own, a getaway where you can retreat, relax, refresh, and rejuvenate? Maybe it's your bedroom, your study, or your bath. For me, as I mentioned, it's my great-mom's rocking chair, located in a tranquil part of my living room. It's just a little corner where I can relax over a cup of coffee as I reflect on what has been and muse over what will be. Even a little bit of time alone can make a bad mood better or enliven an exhausted mom enough to help her endure the rest of her day.

I remember when I was around the age of eight, I designed my own little secret hideout under our basement stairs. We had seven people living under one tiny roof, so having your own space was almost impossible. In fact, it would have been impossible had I not moved the Christmas boxes just enough to create my own little haven of privacy. To make it just right, I incorporated a few of my favorite things—Mrs. Beasley (my doll), my own private candy stash, and a picture of Donny Osmond. Even way back when, I liked having a place to myself where I could chill out and ignore the rest of the world.

Where do you retreat? Where do you go to re-energize and re-establish yourself? If you don't have a special spot, you can create one!

- Pick a place where you can be alone. It might be another room, a corner of a room, a porch—or even a spot under the basement stairs!

- Dejunk the area. Get rid of the clutter so that when you sit down to relax, you can do so without looking around at what needs to be done.

- Gather up a few of your favorite things. Having them around will make the space personal. Items might include family photos, notes of encouragement, artwork, books, or a favorite trinket.

- Keep a comfy pillow and throw nearby, and maybe even a pair of slippers, as well as a journal and a pen.

- If you like music, quietly play your favorite tunes.

- Drink from a fine china cup and saucer or a pretty fluted piece of crystal.

- Indulge in a piece of chocolate or some other little treat.

Now sit back and rest for a spell. Take a moment to relax your body, refresh your mind, and rejuvenate your soul.

MakeOver Minute #78
BREAK OUT

"I don't have the confidence to do anything," the young woman told me. "It's my face—it's so ugly." Her face was badly scarred and pitted with acne. She went on to tell me she was only 19 and had quit school when she was 17 because she'd been teased and tormented mercilessly about her face. "I've always wanted to be a nutritionist, and now I can't do anything because I don't even have a high-school education. I'm too afraid to go back and try. What can I do? How can I move on?"

Unfortunately, this gal's story is all too common. Many of us subconsciously tell ourselves we're not good enough to do what God is calling us to. We don't know how to break out and break away from our past, so we let it keep us from fulfilling our future.

We forget that God not only forgives the past, but uses it to His glory. As an example, the woman I met at the speaking engagement was able to break free from her past and move confidently toward her future. She is now a dietician. God is continuing a good work in her, and she's using what's she's been through to shape upcoming generations.

There has never been the slightest
doubt in my mind that the God who started this great work in
you would keep at it and bring it to a flourishing finish on
the very day Christ Jesus appears.

—Philippians 1:6

Prayer and Praise / Thankful Thoughts: _____

_____

_____

_____

Acne at any age is irritating. In order to keep breakouts at bay you need to institute a good skin-care routine and stick with it. However, even if you practice proper skin care twice a day, you still can get blemishes. In that event, try some of these at-home remedies for on-the-spot treatment.

- **Change your pillowcases** at least once a week. Oil and dirt gather on them and spread to your face as you sleep.

- If you break out on your back, **wash it with antibacterial dish soap.** Dish soap is formulated to cut grease and grime and generally costs less than skin-cleansing products.

- If you don't have blemish ointment handy, **try a dab of mint toothpaste.** Make sure it is paste and not gel.

- **Apply tea tree oil** directly to the spot you want to clear up. Don't use it on your entire face because it's extremely drying and can damage your skin.

- When you get a zit, **zap it with a dab of peroxide** on a cotton swab.

- **Drink lots of water, exercise, and eat a well-balanced diet.** Water helps keep your skin supple, exercise brings oxygen to your cells, and a balanced diet gives you healthy skin.

- **Mix finely grated orange or lemon peel with water to make a thick paste and apply it** to the affected area. Let it sit for five to seven minutes, then rinse.

- **Ice down larger pimples** for 30 seconds before you go to bed. By morning, they will be less red and swollen.

- **Blot oil from your face** using blotting papers or tissues. Do not rub. This will also prevent your foundation from caking when you experience breakthrough shine.

- **Try over-the-counter creams and cleansers** that contain benzoyl peroxide, salicylic acid, and sulfur.

When in doubt about any acne treatment, consult a medical professional.

MakeOver Minute #79
THE MANE EVENT

One of my favorite passages of Scripture has to do with hair care, but not the kind you might think! It has to do with hair that provided care for the Messiah (see Luke 7:36-50).

The woman in this story was thought to be a prostitute, and the fact that she demonstrated such faith and courage as to enter the house of a Pharisee shows us that her love for God outweighed her circumstances. It doesn't say exactly how she entered, but I imagine she knocked on the door and, when it was opened, she spotted the Master across the room. Overcome with emotion, she pushed her way in and fell at Jesus' feet, weeping uncontrollably. Scripture tells us that she cried enough to wash Jesus' feet with her tears and then, having no towel, was resourceful—as most women are—and let down her hair to dry them. She then kissed His feet and anointed them with expensive perfume.

One of the Pharisees, named Simon, was appalled by her actions. Jesus was aware of what he was thinking, and he told Simon a story:

> *"A man loaned money to two people—five hundred pieces of silver to one and fifty pieces to the other. But neither of them could repay him, so he kindly forgave them both, canceling their debts. Who do you suppose loved him more after that?" Simon answered, "I suppose the one for whom he canceled the larger debt." "That's right," Jesus said.*
>
> —Luke 7:41-43 NLT

How much do you love Jesus? Do you love Him enough to make Him the main event? If so, let down your hair and start demonstrating your faith in all you say and do.

Prayer and Praise / Thankful Thoughts: _____

_____

_____

_____

From an early age, we're taught to brush our teeth and hair every single day. My mother used to go through the same routine every morning: "Did you brush?" I realized early on that I'd better brush my hair—and not just "brush *at* it," as Mom would say—because if I didn't, she would. Whether Mom knew it or not, she taught me way back when to take care of my own hair, and I've been keeping it up ever since.

Hair care is a mane event each and every day. There's no escaping it, but you *can* make it easier by getting a good cut, using the right styling products, and knowing a few hair-care secrets.

1. Use several different shampoos and conditioners for your hair type. Alternate them every time you wash your hair to keep it looking clean and fresh. Also remember to thoroughly rinse your hair after you shampoo and condition it so you're not left with dull, limp hair.

2. Add fragrance to your hair by spritzing your favorite scent on a hairbrush and brushing it through your hair.

3. When you blow-dry your hair, hang your head upside down and blast it with the cool setting for the last 60 seconds or so to cool down the hair follicles and increase volume.

4. A crisscross part in your hair will add pizzazz to your do and help hide a needed color touchup.

5. Avoid "bed head" by sleeping on a satin pillowcase.

6. When your hair goes flat, sprinkle your roots with baby powder, turn your head upside down, and shake it with your fingertips so the powder works its way down the shafts. Flip your head up and spritz with the hairspray.

7. Clean your hairbrush and comb by removing the hair first, then soaking them in a hot shampoo bath for five minutes. Rinse and let dry.

8. Control flyaway hair by spraying a hairbrush with hairspray and then gently brushing your hair.

9. Give volume to long hair by partially drying it, then pulling it up on top of your head and securing it with a thick elastic hair band. Next, finish blow-drying your hair, making sure the root area is totally dry.

10. Try this recipe for shiny hair: Mash up one small avocado and combine it with one tablespoon of olive oil and one teaspoon of baking powder. Massage this mixture into your hair and let it sit for 15 minutes. Rinse thoroughly, shampoo, and condition.

MakeOver Minute #80
A WOMAN'S INTUITION

A woman's intuition is her uncanny ability to sense a situation without prior knowledge or evidence. There's nothing mystical or magical about it—it's simply a gut reaction that causes you to have second thoughts about something or see beyond the surface appearance. It's called discernment, and it's God's way of providing guidance to those who are alert to His prompting.

As Christians, the Holy Spirit of God leads us, and it is the Holy Spirit who makes us intuitive. He gives us spiritual insight into what's right and what's wrong.

Not all Christians, however, stay in sync with God. Some become callous to the Holy Spirit's leading. The fact is, to be led by the Spirit of God, you must rely on His guidance and follow His lead every step of the way.

If we are living now by the Holy Spirit, let us follow the Holy Spirit's leading in every part of our lives.

—Galatians 5:25 NLT

To be certain you're being led by God and not by a misguided spirit, always make sure the instruction lines up with the Scriptures. God will never, ever contradict Himself.

The word of God is full of living power. It is sharper than the sharpest knife, cutting deep into our innermost thoughts and desires. It exposes us for what we really are.

—Hebrews 4:12 NLT

Prayer and Praise / Thankful Thoughts: _____

_____

_____

_____

Call it whatever you want—women's intuition, a gut feeling, a sixth sense, or your subconscious—but the fact is, most men and women possess it, even though men rarely use it.

A few years ago, a man from the FBI came to talk to our Officers' Wives Club about being a "woman aware." He instructed us on various self-defense techniques, but stressed that the greatest safeguard we possess as women is our intuition. He said that men have it but are typically too macho to pay attention to it. The statistics he shared showed that men are much more likely to end up in altercations than women because they hardly ever pay attention to their gut feelings. Women, on the other hand, avoid such situations by listening to the warning bells that go off inside them when a situation isn't right.

We used to live out in the countryside, and one time when I was home alone, a strange man knocked on my door. It was brutally cold outside, and the man said his truck had broken down. He asked if he could use my phone. I said, "Just a minute," then closed and locked the door behind me before I went to get my cordless phone. When I returned and offered him the phone through the chained door, he refused, turned away, and left. I had a gut feeling that this man would have forced his way in had the presence of my large dog not scared him away. I went up to a second-story window and watched him walk down the road, get into his truck, and drive off. At that point, I called the police, who informed me they were looking for this man because he'd robbed and had assaulted another woman living in a rural area. Any other time I would have invited this man in—especially given the fact that it was freezing outside—but this time I didn't because something inside told me not to.

Friends, pay attention to your gut! God gives us these feelings for a reason. If something seems wrong, choose to be safe rather than sorry. According to the FBI agent who spoke to our group, statistics show that nine times out of ten, a woman's intuition is correct.

MakeOver Minute #81
SISTER ACT

Two of the most famous sisters in the Bible are Jesus' friends Mary and Martha, the sisters of Lazarus.

> *As Jesus and the disciples continued on their way to Jerusalem, they came to a village where a woman named Martha welcomed them into her home. Her sister, Mary, sat at the Lord's feet, listening to what he taught. But Martha was worrying over the big dinner she was preparing. She came to Jesus and said, "Lord, doesn't it seem unfair to you that my sister just sits here while I do all the work? Tell her to come and help me."*
>
> *But the Lord said to her, "My dear Martha, you are so upset over all these details! There is really only one thing worth being concerned about. Mary has discovered it—and I won't take it away from her."*
>
> —Luke 10:38-43 NLT

Now, I'm not so sure if Martha really wanted Mary to get up and get busy, or if sibling rivalry had set in and she decided to put Mary down in order to get applauded for all she had done. Either way, Jesus gently responds to her comment without placing blame on her efforts. He simply reminds her of the order of priorities, and that hearing *from* God comes before service *to* God.

And all of us have something to learn from these sisters—lessons we can pass on to our own sisters. Love God. Listen to Him. Learn from Him. Lend a helping hand in service whenever it's appropriate.

Sisters, never get tired of doing good.

—2 Thessalonians 3:13 NLT

Prayer and Praise / Thankful Thoughts: _____

_____

_____

_____

Sisterhood is a beautiful thing, and it's birthed in one of two ways—either through family or through friendship. Both are ties that bind. There are the sisters we're related to and grow up with, and there are those we develop relationships with and grow close to. Either way, whether predetermined or handpicked, sisters satisfy who we are.

I didn't always appreciate my sisters when we were growing up, but once I was married and moved away, I missed them tremendously. Although we live in different parts of the country, we still remain close via phone calls and e-mail messages. My sisters and I love each other, listen to each other, learn from each other, and lend a helping hand to each other.

In the absence of my own siblings, God has given me sisterly friends. These gals share everything with me except the DNA. We're always there for each other in both good times and bad. Several years ago, when I was facing a traumatic family crisis, I don't know what I would have done without my best friend, Beth. She put her own life on hold to help me through mine. Girlfriends like this, though not kin, are sisters in the deepest sense of the word.

Make time to be with your sisters. My sisters and I recently planned a "girls only" getaway, and what a blast we had! We talked till all hours of the night, laughed till we cried, and shopped till we dropped. We reminisced over the past and made future memories. It was so much fun that we're already planning our next adventure. If a vacation is out of the question, have a girl's night in. Host a sleepover. Put on your pj's, pop some corn, place an order for pizza, pour some soda pop, and put in a chick flick. Remember, the goal isn't where you go or what you do, but who you do it with. It's all about having sister time.

Sister, act! Take time right now to appreciate that special sister who loves you no matter what, supports you through thick and thin, encourages you to be your best, kindheartedly instructs you, and always lifts you up in prayer. Call, write, or e-mail her, and make a date to strengthen the sisterhood.

MakeOver Minute #82
CLEAN IT OUT

Cleaning out always makes me feel like I've accomplished something significant. Whether I've cleaned out the back of my closet or the depths of my heart, a fresh start always does wonders for who I am on the outside *and* the inside.

Many of us have lives that are a cluttered mess, but before we clear out clothes, we need to clean out our hearts. We need to invite Jesus in to make a clean sweep of our souls.

> *Behold, I stand at the door, and knock: if any man hear my voice, and open the door, I will come in to him, and will sup with him, and he with me.*
> —Revelation 3:20 KJV

Cleaning out both your clothes closet *and* the closet of your heart will give you a fresh lease on life, making way for a new you—both body and soul.

Prayer and Praise / Thankful Thoughts: _____

_____

_____

_____

Open at your own risk. Should this message be posted on your closet door? When was the last time you cleaned out your closet? Can you even *imagine* what's buried in the back? Just recently, I started this arduous process in preparation for a move, and you can't believe some of the things I found—everything from shoes with broken heels to blouses waiting for new buttons. I even located several things I thought I'd lost for good—a pearl necklace, which was draped on a hanger, and my favorite sweater, which I'd blamed my daughter for taking with her to college. When I finished cleaning, it was almost like I'd acquired a whole new wardrobe. Between items rediscovered and items refurbished, the time spent cleaning proved to be quite rewarding!

When you start cleaning out, you need to decide what stays and what goes. Begin by identifying the last time you actually wore the item. If you haven't worn it for a year or more, chances are you never will—so get rid of it. The only exception to this rule is formal wear, and you'll have to decide if you think you'll ever wear it again. After that, consider whether or not the item fits and is flattering to your figure. If it doesn't meet both requirements, it's gotta go.

Next, gather three containers and label them *refuse*, *resale*, and *restore*.

- **Refuse:** Trash it! I don't know how many times I've saved T-shirts with holes, ratty jeans, or worn-out sweats, thinking I'd wear them to paint in or something. The fact is, I never do. These items just take up much-needed closet space. Or what about that item with a stain on it, or the one with sentimental value attached? I once came across an old camp shirt. I never wore the thing, but I felt compelled to keep it because everyone at the camp had signed it. I decided to keep the memory but toss the shirt.

- **Resale:** Items you no longer want—but are still in good condition—go in this container. Write down each item, adding a fair dollar amount as you go, so you can cash in on the tax benefit associated with charitable contributions. Many outstanding organizations would welcome your castoffs. Ask a nearby church for suggestions, or look in the phone book for local charities.

- **Restore:** Put articles of clothing here that are awaiting a trip to the dry cleaner or a quick fix—a sewed-on button, a mended hem—in this container, and attend to their needs as soon as you're done cleaning out. Keep in mind that you can also refurbish items by adding new buttons, beads, or bows. You can also take a dingy white shirt and spiff it up by dyeing it a new color.

For most of us, it's not a matter of having enough clothes to wear—it's a matter of cleaning out and rediscovering what we already own. It's all about getting rid of the clothing clutter and keeping those items that look good, fit right, and feel great. Cleaning out your closet never fails to give you a fresh start!

MakeOver Minute #83
TOP IT OFF

When you accessorize, you take the basic and make it better. Accessorizing is what sets us apart as individuals. It's what makes us unique, not only in how we adorn our outer environment, but also how we enhance our lives from the inside out. According to Galatians 5:22-23, Christians are called to lead out-of-the-ordinary lives. God, through His Word, inspires us to be different—to pull our lives together by adding the special effects of the fruit of the Spirit to our everyday living.

Love, joy, peace, patience, kindness, goodness, faithfulness, gentleness, and self-control, add just the right touch of uniformity in Christ without taking away from your own individuality. When you accessorize yourself with the fruit of the Spirit, you'll beautify the environment in which you live and be like a shining star in the dark part of the world in which you reside.

When the Holy Spirit controls our lives, he will produce this kind of fruit in us: love, joy, peace, patience, kindness, goodness, faithfulness, gentleness, and self-control.

—Galatians 5:22-23 NLT

Prayer and Praise / Thankful Thoughts: _____

_____

_____

_____

Fashion accessories are just what you need to fix up an old wardrobe or put the finishing touches on a new one. Unfortunately, we often forget about accessories and fail to factor them into our clothing budget, even though they can make or break an outfit. Why invest in a new pair of pants, blouse, and jacket if you're not going to pull them together with the right accessories?

Accessories can change everything. I have an inexpensive little black dress that I purchased a number of years ago, and it never goes out of style because I'm always updating it with new accessories. It's so versatile—I can dress it up or down, depending on what I put with it. When I want to go casual, I pair it with a sarong or leggings. If I want to class it up a little, I wear it with a beaded jacket, fine jewelry, and high heels. Either way, it looks great—in fact, it doesn't even look like I'm wearing the same dress!

Building an outfit is a lot like making an ice-cream sundae. Most sundaes begin with plain old vanilla ice cream and are made to order from there. You might choose hot fudge, caramel, a banana, and whipped cream. Or you may prefer swirls of strawberry, crushed pineapple, and toasted coconut. Either way, it's yours to enjoy!

Our wardrobes are also put together to suit our own individual tastes. Two gals could purchase the exact same thing and achieve two very different styles depending on how they top it off. The little extras are what give clothing that personal touch. Get ready to update an outfit you already have or start up one you plan to purchase. Either way, accessorizing will make you look like all that and more, with the cherry on top!

- **Belt to buckles:** Current trends in the belt and buckle department can keep you stylish without breaking the bank. Be sure to match belts and buckles to your size and shape. A thick belt on a petite gal will make her look shorter, just as a thin belt on a tall girl will make her appear taller. Modification is the key.

- **Jewelry to jackets:** Costume jewelry changes each season, so buy only a few inexpensive and interchangeable pieces to work with. Another great accessorizing tool is a stylish jacket—one that can be worn over different outfits in order to add a bit of fashionable flair.

- **Hair to heels:** Don't forget about your hair—it's one of your greatest accessories! Whether you do it up or leave it down, beautiful hair works wonders for your overall appearance. The size and shape of the heel on your shoe can also add or detract from your outfit. Rule of thumb—the shorter the skirt, the flatter the heel—and vice versa.

- **Eyeglasses to eye shadow:** Trendy eyeglasses and eye shadow shades add just the right amount of eye candy to complete any look.

MakeOver Minute #84
SHARPER IMAGE

Your outward appearance is one thing, but who you are beneath the surface depicts the *real* you—and the real you is patterned after the bare essentials of size, shape, and style.

1. **Size** up what the Word of God says. Bible study will give you insight into everyday life. To get started, here's a topical approach that works for me. I call it the 6-R method—**r**ead, w**r**ite, **r**esearch, **r**elate, **r**equest, and **r**emember. Select a topic and use a concordance to jot down verses pertaining to that topic, then apply the 6-R method: *read* the verse, *write* the verse, *research* the same verse in other Bible translations, *relate* it to yourself personally, *request* additional insight through prayer, and *remember* it by either memorizing the Scripture or meditating on it.

2. **Shape** yourself in the glory of the Spirit, and how you respond to life will be fittingly balanced. Our lives are wrought by trials and adversity. It's been said, life is 10 percent what happens to us and 90 percent how we react to it. You can either be reactive or proactive in your approach. A reactive response is done in the flesh, but a proactive approach follows the Spirit's prompting through prayer and Scripture application.

3. **Style** your life after that of Christ. He is your perfect model. When you begin to understand and apply the truth about Christ to your own life, it will transform you morally, and the more closely you follow after Him, the more like Him you will become.

Our faces are not covered. They show the bright glory of the Lord, as the Lord's Spirit makes us more and more like our glorious Lord.

—2 Corinthians 3:18 CEV

Prayer and Praise / Thankful Thoughts: _____

_____

_____

_____

It's time to talk about the bare essentials. What you wear underneath it all affects how you look from the inside out and from the bottom up. Your size, shape, and style determine the type of undergarments you'll need in order to visually create a balanced body.

1. **Size:** The most common mistake made when purchasing bras and panties is choosing the wrong size. To find your correct bra size, see "MakeOver Minute #23," and to pick the perfect panties, simply buy the same size as your pants.

2. **Shape:** Your body shape determines the type of underwear you should wear. The goal is to bring balance to your figure, and certain styles are better than others for your body type.

   - If you have a *triangle*-shaped figure, the goal is to achieve balance between your top and your bottom. A fully padded bra will lift your breasts, helping to create fullness on top. Seamless control panties will minimize your lower half.

   - If you have a *wedge*-shaped figure, you'll want to put together a look of softness and enhance the visual curve of your bustline with an underwire bra and comfy boy-short-style underwear.

   - Add natural-looking curves to a *rectangle*-shaped figure by enhancing your bustline. A push-up bra will enhance your figure without making it look ill-proportioned. Choose half-bikini or low-rise briefs.

   - If you have an *hourglass* figure, a full-coverage bra supports the natural shape of your breasts without diminishing your natural curves. Seamless tummy-control panties work best for this shape.

   - *Circle*-shaped gals are usually well-endowed. If this is true of you, wear a bra that offers maximum coverage in all areas—including the area beneath your armpits. Choose full-figure panties that fit well without riding up.

3. **Style:** Some articles of clothing require special types of underwear. For instance, you might need a strapless or an athletic bra, depending on your attire. Or maybe your outfit calls for shaper underwear to camouflage extra belly fat.

You'll notice immediately how wearing the right undergarments has a positive effect on your overall appearance. The perfect size, shape, and style of underwear not only enhances your figure, but also improves the fit of your clothes so you can project a sharper image.

MakeOver Minute #85
TAKE FIVE

Just as a five-minute makeover might seem impossible, the disciples didn't believe that five loaves of bread and two fishes were adequate either. They didn't realize that Jesus was, is, and always will be the great provider.

Jesus took the five loaves and two fish, looked up toward heaven, and asked God's blessing on the food. Breaking the loaves into pieces, he kept giving the bread and fish to the disciples to give to the people. They all ate as much as they wanted, and they picked up twelve baskets of leftovers!

—Luke 9:16-17 NLT

Jesus multiplied five loaves and two fish to feed more than 5000 people. This measly amount seemed insufficient to the disciples, but in the hands of God it became more than enough.

Not that we are sufficient of ourselves to think of anything as being from ourselves, but our sufficiency is from God.

—2 Corinthians 3:5 NKJV

When you are faced with a seemingly impossible task, do what you can and ask God to do the rest. He can bless and use whatever you bring Him, whether it be time, talent, or treasure. God can do—and will do—great miracles with what little you have. Allow Jesus to multiply your gifts, and you'll be blessed by the leftovers!

Prayer and Praise / Thankful Thoughts: _____

_____

_____

_____

Your face is your main point of communication, so how you look from the neck up is important. One day after working out at the gym, I decided to buzz by the grocery store to pick up a couple things, which was my first mistake. Doesn't it figure, the only time I didn't have on any makeup and my hair was uncombed, I seemed to run into everyone I know! To add insult to injury, one of the gals I ran into had just been to a seminar I'd presented about always looking your best, and I could tell I lost all credibility right there on the spot. From that day on, I've learned how to pull myself together in just five minutes. So whether I'm running late or I'm just on my way home from the gym, I'm committed to communicating a pulled-together look in hardly any time at all.

5-minute makeup:

1. In just one minute, you can...
   - freshen your face with a baby wipe.
   - rub in moisturizer containing an SPF.
   - apply foundation. (For a quick fix, use a one-step formula that combines liquid coverage with a powdery finish.)
2. In the second minute, you can...
   - apply and blend in blusher.
   - spread on a neutral eye shadow.
   - apply eyeliner, concentrating on the corners of your eyes. (A self-sharpening style pencil is most convenient for saving time.)
3. In the third minute, you can...
   - brush brows into place. (Skip the brow pencil unless your brows are in desperate need of color.)
   - apply mascara to lashes.
4. In the fourth minute, you can...
   - apply lip color.
   - brush your hair.
5. In the fifth minute, you can...
   - pull long hair back into a ponytail and slick short hair back with hair gel.
   - put on a baseball cap. (I bought a couple of cute caps with studs and sequins for this very occasion.)
   - add a pair of trendy earrings.

Always be prepared by keeping everything you need in a single bag. This way you can dump it, use it, and put it back in a matter of minutes.

MakeOver Minute #86
EXCESS BAGGAGE

If you wish to travel far and fast, travel light. Take off all your envies, jealousies, unforgiveness, selfishness, and fears.

—Glenn Clark

Travel can be exhausting when you have to lug around excess baggage. Extra weight bogs you down and makes getting from place to place much more difficult. How true this same scenario is in life! When you are weighed down with feelings such as envy, jealousy, unforgiveness, selfishness, and fear, life can be overwhelming at best. And when these emotions are left unattended, they can snowball into feelings that are even worse—hate, bitterness, anger, callousness, panic, and worry, which only add to the extreme weight of the burden. Experience has taught me that unless I deal with oppressive issues head-on, it's hard to move on. So let's learn to unpack these emotions, get rid of the excess baggage, and get on with life!

Confess your sins to each other and pray for each other so that you may be healed. The earnest prayer of a righteous person has great power and wonderful results.

—James 5:16 NLT

Create in me a clean heart, O God, And renew a steadfast spirit within me.

—Psalm 51:10 NKJV

Prayer and Praise / Thankful Thoughts:_____

_____

_____

_____

We live in a very transient society. What with frequent business trips and in-between getaways, it seems like we're always heading off somewhere. I, for one, thoroughly enjoy traveling, but the one thing I *don't* like is all the packing and the unpacking associated with the event. It's always been a challenge for me because I tend to overpack. However, a little practical advice combined with lots of practice has forced me to become somewhat of a packing professional. Experience has taught me how to save time, utilize space, and even score some free cosmetics in the process!

- **Pack less.** Begin by laying out everything you think you'll need, then pare it down from there. As I was packing for my China trip, I discovered I'd laid out no less than 32 shirts. Now granted, it was a six-week adventure, but I still didn't need that many tops! By the time I was done eliminating, I had just 17 shirts—about half of what I'd started with.

- **Pack sensibly.** Mix and match your travel wardrobe. Make sure every piece of clothing you pack works with every other piece so you can create a variety of possible looks. Quite often, I take only one pair of black pants with several tops to match. This tactic also cuts back on the number of shoes I need to pack.

- **Pack light.** Pack travel-size toiletries. There's no reason to tote around full-size bottles when you can get by with much less. It's also possible to get these items for free if you plan ahead. When I go to the hair salon or makeup counter, I always collect freebees. Shampoo packets are a great alternative to bottles, and sample-size cosmetics get the job done without taking up very much space. Place these essentials in heavy-duty plastic zip-lock bags to protect against leaks and, if possible, pack them in the outer pockets of your luggage. Also use the outer pockets for your hairbrush, comb, and styling utensils. I also save time by keeping my toiletries packed at all times. They're always in my suitcase, ready to go at a moment's notice.

- **Pack smart.** Rolling your clothes will save space and keep wrinkles at bay. Lay two or three items on top of one another, smooth to flatten, then roll them as you would a sleeping bag. Place rolled items in your suitcase first, then fold stiffer items—like jeans—in half and lay them on top. Next, stuff your shoes with socks, hose, or underwear, place them in a shoe bag, and pack them around the border of your suitcase.

- **Pack safe.** For security reasons, do not pack money, jewelry, travel documents (such as your passport), prescription medication, keys, eyeglasses, or other valuables in your luggage. Carry them with you.

Usually, when we refer to someone being in love with himself or herself, we're talking about someone who is conceited. But that's not the case with being faithfully fit. It's one thing to be conceited, but it's totally another thing to be self-confident through a loving relationship with God.

This is a real love. It is not that we loved God, but that He loved us and sent His Son as a sacrifice to take away our sins.

—1 John 4:10 NLT

Because the God of the universe loved you first, you can love and accept who you are because you were created in His image (see Genesis 1:27). As a Christian, God's love for you is unconditional. Do you have that kind of love for yourself?

Prayer and Praise / Thankful Thoughts: _____

_____

_____

_____

One day I telephoned one of the top modeling agencies in the world and asked, "What is the number-one quality you look for in a potential model?" To my surprise, it wasn't height, weight, or fabulous hair—it was faith! You must have faith, thick skin, and self-confidence in endless amounts to enter the harsh world of modeling. The answer surprised me at first, but once I stopped to think about it, it made total sense. With this occupation comes a seemingly endless amount of rejection, which requires inner strength to survive.

All of us have been faced with rejection of some sort. Maybe you've been rejected by your parents, your spouse, a family member, a friend, or an employer. It happens to us all. The secret to overcoming rejection lies in having faith in yourself. If you're constantly finding yourself on the outs, take a look inside. Chances are, you'll discover you don't like yourself, and when you don't accept and respect yourself, others usually won't either.

To like yourself and to deal with rejection in a positive manner, you must be all that you can be physically, emotionally, relationally, mentally, and spiritually. When you stay faithfully committed to improving all aspects of your life, you'll feel better about yourself, and this confidence will give you the strength to carry on.

- Your **emotional health** affects your overall sense of worth. Emotional insecurity can make you bitter, which leads to a negative spirit. Healthy emotional understanding, on the other hand, can see the positive spin in just about anything, allowing you the ability to find the silver lining in the darkest of days.

- **Spiritual strength** comes from having a personal relationship with Jesus Christ. It's all about finding acceptance in Him alone. Your soul is the source of purpose, significance, and inner peace. It's the most inward part of your being—it drives your convictions, actions, and thoughts, which in turn drive your faith in God and confidence in the fact that God loves and accepts you no matter what.

- **Physical care** boosts confidence. Take time to look your best, and you will be more secure in who you are as an individual.

- **Mental strength** is power. Never stop learning. Keep up on current events, take a class, or learn a new skill—whatever the case, give your brain an assignment. Make it work for a living.

- **Relational ties** between family, friends, co-workers, and peers influence us for good or bad. These people can make you feel better or worse about yourself, depending on the status of your relationship. In some circumstances, it's within your realm of control to make a stressed relationship better, but in cases where it isn't, you must prayerfully let it go.

It's never too late to be a super (role) model. You too can demonstrate that it's possible to have faith in oneself by being your best emotionally, spiritually, physically, mentally, and relationally. With this attitude rejection won't get you down—it will just make you strive harder the next time.

MakeOver Minute #88
LASH OUT

When we think about "lashing out," extending eyelashes is one thing, but lashing out with your tongue has a totally different effect. While false eyelashes extend, the spreading of false information exploits and destroys lives. Most of us are no strangers to gossip. We've all been affected by it in one way or another—we've spread it, listened to it, or been the subject of it.

To fear the LORD is to hate evil; I hate pride and arrogance, evil behavior and perverse speech.

—Proverbs 8:13 NIV

Don't get swept away in gossip, because once you lash out, you can never take it back. Words wound. Yes, they can be forgiven, but the scars they leave behind have long-lasting effects.

Complain if you must, but don't lash out. Keep your mouth shut, and let your heart do the talking.

—Psalm 4:4

Prayer and Praise / Thankful Thoughts: _____

_____

_____

_____

All you have to do is bat your eyelashes. How many times have you heard this said, suggesting that this action will get you whatever you want? Maybe that's why so many of us wish for long, lush beauties to flutter from our lids. While few of us are blessed with intensely long, thick eyelashes, it *is* possible to have them with just the wave of a wand.

There are a vast variety of mascaras on the market, each with different additives and applicators designed to do a variety of things. To know which type of mascara is right for your lashes, you need only consider two things—kind and color.

- **Kind:** What do you want your mascara to do for you? Do you want it to lengthen, volumize, curl, condition, or color? Also, do you need waterproof or regular? There's not much difference between formulas, but there are differences in the applicators. Different shaped mascara wands do different things. A full-bristle brush will lengthen, separate, and feather lashes without clumping. An eyelash comb will separate, sculpt, and define shorter lashes.

- **Color:** Classic mascara colors are brown, brown-black, and black, but mascara also comes in an array of trendy shades. To apply colored mascara, first apply one coat of your regular mascara, then follow up with a second coat of the colored mascara. This method will intensify your lashes while adding just a hint of color.

While applying mascara is pretty simple, a few helpful techniques will let your lashes reach their full potential.

1. The first step to having beautiful lashes is curling them. Use an eyelash curler on your upper lashes *before* you apply mascara. Open the curler and place your upper lashes in the opening, positioning the curler at the root. With a steady hand, gently squeeze the curler shut, hold for ten seconds, and release.

2. Unscrew your mascara and slowly twist the brush around to coat the bristles. Don't pump the wand up and down, which pushes air into the tube and dries out the mascara.

3. Apply the mascara by positioning the brush at the base of your upper lashes and gently sweeping upward to the tips. Repeat this process on your lower lashes. To avoid clumping, apply a second coat of mascara before the first coat dries.

4. To remove flakes and clumps, use a clean mascara brush to sweep through your lashes. I keep a clean wand from an empty mascara tube just for this purpose.

5. Clean up smudges with a cotton swab. Prevent smudging by applying a light dusting of translucent powder.

Use eye-safe makeup remover to clean off all traces of mascara. Before you go to bed, prick a vitamin E gel capsule with a sterile needle. Squeeze out the gel and gently massage it into your lashes. This will condition your lashes while you sleep.

MakeOver Minute #89
PLANNING FOR THAT SPECIAL EVENT

There is a wedding we've all been invited to—not as the guest, but as the honored bride of Christ.

> *You husbands must love your wives with the same love*
> *Christ showed the church. He gave up his life for her to make her*
> *holy and clean, washed by baptism and God's word.*
> *He did this to present her to himself as a glorious church*
> *without a spot or wrinkle or any other blemish. Instead,*
> *she will be holy and without fault.*
>
> —Ephesians 5:25-27 NLT

Once you accept the proposal, the preparation begins. Like a bride making wedding plans, we are preparing to join our groom in glory. To fully understand this analogy, we must go back in time and take a look at Jewish culture. A Jewish wedding started with an agreement between the fathers, and was then followed by a public engagement. The engagement period would last about a year, during which time the bridegroom would return to his family home to prepare a place for his bride.

> *In my Father's house are many rooms; if it were not so, I would*
> *have told you. I am going there to prepare a place for you. And if*
> *I go and prepare a place for you, I will come back and take you*
> *to be with me that you also may be where I am.*
>
> —John 14:2-3 NIV

Meanwhile, the bride would prepare herself for the ceremony, which would be about a year away, although she never knew the exact date. As the bride, she had to be ready for her groom's return at a moment's notice. When he came, a groomsman would sound the shofar (a ram's-horn trumpet) to announce the bridegroom's arrival, and the entire wedding party would gather at the bride's house—along with the bride, who was ready to attend the wedding feast with her groom.

> *Let us be glad and rejoice and honor him. For the time*
> *has come for the wedding feast of the Lamb,*
> *and his bride has prepared herself.*
>
> —Revelation 19:7 NLT

Christ is the bridegroom, and you are part of His bride, the church. He is making preparations for you, but are you ready to meet Him? Waiting and preparing for Christ, the bridegroom, is a daily process of focusing on Him as you study God's Word, pray, and share the joy of your engagement with others. When the bridegroom comes, be ready—this will be the main event!

Stay alert. You have no idea when he might arrive.

—Matthew 25:13

I promised to give you to Christ, as your only husband. I want to give you as his pure bride.

—2 Corinthians 11:2 NCV

Prayer and Praise / Thankful Thoughts: _____

_____

_____

_____

Special occasions require advance preparation! When you consider what all you may need—a new dress, hose, cosmetics, lingerie, nail care, and hair care—you can quickly see how scheduling and budgeting are of the essence.

Before you start making plans, ask yourself a few questions. First, what is the event? Second, what is the dress code? **A black-tie affair** requires formal attire—tuxedos for the gentleman and long dresses or dressy evening separates for the ladies. **Black-tie optional** means that the man has the option of wearing a tux, with a simple cocktail dress acceptable for the woman. Let's look at some more terms:

- **White-tie or ultraformal:** Full dress for the gentlemen with white tie, vest, and shirt; long, dressy gowns with gloves optional for the ladies.

- **Creative black-tie:** Trendy interpretations of formal wear are the rule here! A more modern tux with a colored shirt is acceptable for him, and dressy casual separates—such as a silk skirt and sequined top—are just the things for her.

- **Semiformal:** A dark suit and conservative tie for him, and a short dress or dressy suit for her.

- **Cocktail attire:** A dark suit with a conservative tie for him, a short, elegant dress for her.

- **Dressy casual** or **business casual:** No jeans or shorts!

- **Casual** or **informal:** This generally means that anything goes, but do consider the event. An outdoor picnic is one thing, but an outdoor wedding is entirely different. In the case of the latter, decorum should prevail—casual for him would be a nice pair of slacks and a button-down shirt, while casual for her would be a dress or nice slacks and a dressy top.

First things first! Don't forget to RSVP, and schedule hair, nail, makeup, and pedicure appointments right away because calendars book up fast, especially around prom time or the holidays.

Now, it's time to focus on the outfit. The single most important bit of advice I can give you is to choose something that makes you feel beautiful and special. The trick is to utilize clothing, accessories, makeup, and hair to your advantage. Play up your assets and conceal your weak areas to put the focus on *you,* not what you're wearing. You—not your wardrobe—should stand out. Here are a few more things to think about:

- The "LBD"—little black dress—is always an acceptable pick unless it's a formal event or a daytime wedding.

- Shoes should look good, but make sure they're comfortable enough that you're able to enjoy the event.

- Don't skimp on grooming. Makeup, perfume, and hair can make or break your special occasion.

- If you have a tight budget, borrow things like accessories from a friend.

- Match your undergarments to your dress. Also, don't be embarrassed to buy a body slimmer or shaper underwear if you need it.

- Classic furs or faux furs always offer a timeless touch of elegance.

- Use accessories to accent. Don't get caught up in too much of a good thing. Remember—the goal is to make you look great, not garish.

- If you're not sure whether or not to wear pantyhose, try alternatives such as fishnet stockings, toeless hose (for toeless shoes), or self-tanner.

Give yourself plenty of time to get ready on the day of the event. Make the preparation time as special as the occasion and, most of all, enjoy yourself. It's not often you get to feel this pretty!

MakeOver Minute #90
CLEANSE HER

The first step to a good-looking face is proper skin care. Even before you apply cosmetics, you need to clean your skin in order to get a glowing complexion. The key is in the cleansing process. Cleansing your soul does for your inside what cleansing your skin does for your outside.

When we are cleansed by the blood of the Lamb, we have the power of God coursing through us, making even the most difficult of circumstances endurable. Just recently, there was a story in the news about a man who publicly forgave his daughter's murderer. His statement went something like this: "Who am I to judge, when I've been forgiven by God? If God in His righteousness can forgive me, I too can forgive." Do you have that kind of soul-cleansing power? If not, what's stopping you from praying to receive it right now?

The blood of Christ cleans up our whole lives, inside and out. Through the Spirit, Christ offered himself as an unblemished sacrifice, freeing us from all those dead-end efforts to make ourselves respectable, so that we can live all out for God.

—Hebrews 9:14-15

Prayer and Praise / Thankful Thoughts: _____

_____

_____

_____

Did you know that your facial skin reveals where you've been and what you've been up to? I can look at a gal's skin and immediately tell whether she spends too much time in the sun, gets sufficient sleep, drinks enough water, smokes, or follows a good skin care routine. All of these things contribute to the condition of your skin.

Quality care is the key to having good-looking skin. Outside of sun, sleep, hydration, and oxygen, *it's a good skin-care routine, cleanser, toner, and moisturizer that will do wonders for the health and appearance of your skin.* To get started, you must identify your skin type so you'll know which type of products you'll need.

- **Dry skin** looks tight, flaky, and dull in appearance. Choose an extra-creamy cleanser, an alcohol-free toner, and a moisturizer rich in emollients.

- **Normal skin** is what we all wish for: not too dry, not too oily, but—as Goldilocks said—"just right." Care for normal skin with a water-soluble cleanser, mild toner, and a light moisturizer.

- **Oily skin** tends to have large pores, appears greasy, and breaks out frequently. The best treatment for oily skin is a water-based cleanser, an alcohol-based toner, and a lightweight, oil-free moisturizer. Remember, even if your skin is oily, it still needs moisturizer. Treat blemishes with an ointment containing benzoyl peroxide or salicylic acid. Do not use blemish creams on your entire face—treat the problem spot only.

- **Combination skin** is oily in the T-zone (forehead, nose, and chin) and normal to dry everywhere else. Instead of using two different products, look for skin-care products specifically formulated for combination skin. When you wash your face, concentrate on the T-zone area. Your moisturizer should be water-based and contain hydrating properties to soothe and protect the skin's surface.

- **Sensitive skin** reacts adversely to many skin-care and cosmetic products. Hypoallergenic products usually—but not always—work best on sensitive skin. Always test the product in a small area before you use it on your entire face. If your skin is quite problematic, you might consult a dermatologist.

- **Aging skin** appears dry, flaky, and spotty. It lacks firmness and elasticity due to hormonal changes within the body. The best products for this skin type contain alpha hydroxy acids (AHAs), which help eliminate dead cells and increase new skin-cell production.

Skin-care regimens may need to be readjusted for weather changes or during your menstrual cycle. You most likely won't need a whole new routine, but a tweak here or there will be all you need to improve your skin's condition.

MakeOver Minute #91
GRIEF-STRICKEN

In so many ways, death seems so final, but for the believer, death is not the end but only the beginning.

> *We are confident, yes, well pleased rather to be absent from the body and to be present with the Lord.*
>
> —2 Corinthians 5:8 NKJV

At the moment of death, a Christian's soul leaves its earthly body, and immediately comes into the presence of the Lord. Although those left behind do grieve, a homecoming celebration takes place in heaven.

This past year, a very dear friend of mine died in a car accident. Although all who knew her were shocked and grief-stricken over our loss, we took comfort in the fact that she went home to be with Jesus. Her parents, in particular, have displayed great faith as a testament to their hope in God. In fact, her memorial service was less like a funeral and more like a worship celebration.

The Bible tells us that the Thessalonians were curious about death, wondering what happened to fellow Christians who had died and what would happen when Christ returned. Paul, through God's divine inspiration, answered their questions.

> *Regarding the question, friends, that has come up about what happens to those already dead and buried, we don't want you in the dark any longer. First off, you must not carry on over them like people who have nothing to look forward to, as if the grave were the last word. Since Jesus died and broke loose from the grave, God will most certainly bring back to life those who died in Jesus.*
>
> *And then this: We can tell you with complete confidence—we have the Master's word on it—that when the Master comes again to get us, those of us who are still alive will not get a jump on the dead and leave them behind. In actual fact, they'll be ahead of us. The Master himself will give the command. Archangel thunder! God's trumpet blast! He'll come down from*

heaven and the dead in Christ will rise—they'll go first. Then the rest of us who are still alive at the time will be caught up with them into the clouds to meet the Master. Oh, we'll be walking on air! And then there will be one huge family reunion with the Master. So reassure one another with these words.
—1 Thessalonians 4:13-18

These are words of hope and comfort to all who believe. Some day the love that united us here will bring us together for all eternity. Death is only a temporary separation—we'll have all of eternity to make up for lost time. So until then, take care of yourself, comfort each other with these words, and be vigilant in your faith.

I weep with grief; encourage me by your word.
—Psalm 119:28 NLT

Prayer and Praise / Thankful Thoughts: _____
_____
_____
_____

Grief is a very real part of life, and all of us handle it in different ways. When you suffer the loss of a loved one—through death, divorce, or desertion—life may seem meaningless and you may experience feelings of despair for quite some time. Nevertheless, through the process you must continue to take care of yourself and be especially vigilant during the tough times.

My mother recently passed away, and I've been learning firsthand how to manage grief. I won't tell you it's easy—because it never is—but following the advice below will help get you through the tough times.

- **Take care of your physical needs.** Lack of sleep and nourishment will only make you feel worse. Eat small amounts, and make sure your diet includes some type of protein—a bite of cheese, a handful of nuts. Sleeping pills may help for the most restless of nights, but don't use them for a prolonged period of time. Your mind and body need to adjust naturally to bereavement, and sleeping pills inhibit this process—not to mention the fact that they can become addictive. Instead, soak in a hot bath and sip herbal tea just before bedtime.

- **Take time to exercise.** If nothing else, just go for a walk around the block.

- **Be easy on yourself.** Don't set your expectations too high. Give yourself permission to cancel appointments and be disheveled for a few days.

- **Don't make any major decisions too fast or too soon.** Take at least a year to adjust to the loss before you make a move, change jobs, or start a new relationship.

- **Avoid any type of substance abuse**. Don't use alcohol or drugs as a remedy. They never work, and they simply end up adding to the pain.

- **Get away.** Even if it's just for a few hours, go to the cinema and mindlessly watch a movie.

- **Journal your feelings**. Putting your emotions on paper can help you sleep better.

- **Share your pain**. Talking to family members or friends can be helpful, but if these people are too close to the pain themselves, you might want to see a professional counselor.

- **Boost your self-esteem.** If your self-worth has been affected by the loss, find ways to feel better about yourself. Get a makeover, buy a new outfit, and note your achievements, however small they might be. Did you get up and get dressed this morning? Congratulations! That alone is an accomplishment.

- **Take time to reminisce**. On my mom's birthday, I went through old photographs, and read through cards she had sent me. I felt just a little bit closer to her by remembering the good times.

- **Give it time.** The acute pain you feel in the beginning will diminish and life will gradually seem less empty and hopeless. It's only been a few months since my mother died, even though it seems a lot longer than that. I still have those days when I find myself reaching for the phone to give her a call, but they're happening less frequently than they were. At least I have the promise of being with her again in eternity, which means that one day I'll be able to call on her face-to-face.

MakeOver Minute #92
THE GREAT COVER-UP

One of the most infamous cover-up attempts in history is recorded in the Bible:

> *Cain said to his brother Abel, "Let's go out into the field." While they were out in the field, Cain attacked his brother Abel and killed him. Later, the LORD said to Cain, "Where is your brother Abel?" Cain answered, "I don't know. Is it my job to take care of my brother?" Then the LORD said, "What have you done? Your brother's blood is crying out to me from the ground."*
>
> —Genesis 4:8-10 NCV

Cain obviously did not understand the omniscience or omnipresence of God, but we need to. Nothing is hidden from His eyes. Whatever it is you're trying to cover up, you're doing it in vain because God knows all and sees all. Before the situation gets out of control and becomes disastrous, confess it to God, and uncover it to a trusted confidante who will keep you accountable as you work through it. Drugs, alcohol, adulterous affairs via the Internet, cheating on your taxes—whatever the case may be, end the cover-up and present your life as a living sacrifice to God.

> *I confessed all my sins to you and stopped trying to hide them. I said to myself, "I will confess my rebellion to the LORD." And you forgave me! All my guilt is gone.*
>
> —Psalm 32:5 NLT

Prayer and Praise / Thankful Thoughts: _____

_____

_____

_____

A good concealer can cover a multitude of flaws. It's used to hide blemishes, camouflage dark under-eye circles, mask scars, and disguise skin discolorations. It's the one product you'll want to consider, even if you don't normally wear makeup. Blended with foundation or worn alone, it gives you on-the-spot coverage wherever you need it.

Choosing the right formula of concealer is similar to finding the right foundation, but not nearly as confusing. Concealers typically only come in three shades—light, medium, and dark—and you'll want one that is one to two shades lighter than your foundation.

There are a variety of types of concealers on the market—stick, liquid, cream, or medicated. One of the most versatile formulas that's easy to use is an opaque cream concealer. When applied with a concealer brush, this type offers complete coverage.

Apply concealer directly to the area you wish to cover *before* you apply your foundation. This will allow the concealer to briefly set before you smooth on foundation. Blending foundation over the concealer will give your skin a flawless look without highlighting a blemish or creating raccoon eyes. Follow the directions below for foolproof application to specific areas.

1. **Dark circles:** Using your ring finger, gently dab a small amount of concealer under your eye. Gently pat and blend with a makeup sponge or concealer brush.

2. **Blemishes:** First, treat problem spots with a medicated blemish cream. Let it dry for three minutes. Next, use your ring finger to dab a small amount directly on the blemish. Lightly pat on and around the area to blend.

3. **Scratches, scars, and age spots:** Use your ring finger to gently dab concealer onto the affected area. Let dry for one minute, then use a concealer brush or makeup sponge to blend.

4. **Eye-shadow base:** To brighten eyes and give your eye shadow longevity, apply a tiny amount of concealer to your eyelid. Blend it from the base of your lash toward the top of your eyelid. Be careful not to use too much or your eyes will look like spotlights.

5. **Lip-color base:** Use your ring finger to gently pat on a sheer application of concealer before you apply lip color. This will give your lipstick a boost of color as well as help it stay put.

MakeOver Minute #93
BLUSH UP

Blush up—be bold! Take a biblical stand, and let your voice be heard. It's true that following Christ isn't always easy. People are prejudiced against our faith and taunt, tease, and undermine us for it. Though it's a life filled with challenges, in the end, it's all worth it.

> God blesses those who are persecuted because they live for God, for the Kingdom of Heaven is theirs. God blesses you when you are mocked and persecuted and lied about because you are my followers. Be happy about it! Be very glad! For a great reward awaits you in heaven. And remember, the ancient prophets were persecuted, too.
> —Matthew 5:10-12 NLT

You *can* make a difference. Inform yourself on the issues, then look for ways to take action for or against the ones that affect you most. If nothing else, exercise your right to vote or write a letter to the editor of your local newspaper. Use your voice to influence change. Don't cower in the face of rejection. Participation is power, and God is our empowerment—so brush up and take a stand for what you believe in.

> Be strong, be courageous, all you that hope in the LORD.
> —Psalm 31:24 GNT

Prayer and Praise / Thankful Thoughts: _____

_____

_____

_____

Years ago, before the convenience of cosmetic blusher, girls would manage a rosy glow by pinching their cheeks until they were bright red. Now, I don't know about you, but I'm sure happy those days are gone! Now, all we need to achieve a healthy glow is makeup and a brush.

Blusher—or rouge, as some call it—is probably the most difficult of all cosmetics to apply. When you put on too much or fail to blend it, you can look like a clown. When perfectly applied, though, it can enhance your cheekbones, brighten your eyes, and bring color to your complexion.

Like other cosmetics, blush should complement your skin tone without being too bold. To find just the right color, choose a blush from either the warm or cool color family, depending on your skin tone. Next, consider the intensity of the color by judging whether you have a light, medium, or dark complexion. Then choose a couple of colors with which to experiment. Once you find your color, there's only one thing left to decide—cream or powder? I recommend powder because it's much more versatile to use and works for all skin types. Now you're ready!

1. Apply blush following the application of foundation and a dusting of powder. When you apply a powder blush to a powdered face, it will go on smoother without becoming uneven and blotchy. If you are using a cream blush, it should go on after the foundation and before the powder.

2. For a healthy-looking glow, apply blush to your cheekbones. To find your cheekbones, smile to reveal the apples of your cheeks, which is where you naturally blush. Using a blush brush, start at the center of the eye, and sweep the blush upward towards the hairline, stopping at the temple.

3. Apply only a little at a time, repeating the process as necessary. To avoid putting on too much blush, dip your brush in loose powder before you dip into your blusher. The two together will help you blend easier without overdoing it.

4. The key to a natural-looking blush is in the blending, so don't skip this step. To blend, smooth the base of a makeup sponge over the area, removing any line so there is no start or stop to the color.

The sweeping effect of blush not only illuminates your cheekbones, but also gives you an instant facelift by drawing the eye upward toward your own sparkling beauties. So blush up—but when it comes to blusher, less is more. Wearing too little is far better than wearing too much!

MakeOver Minute #94
BEAUTY BENEFITS

Did you know that Christianity has beautiful benefits? There are privileges associated with a believer's position—exclusive advantages reserved for those who have a personal relationship with Jesus Christ.

The number-one beauty benefit of being a Christian is that you've been adopted into the family of God. You're now a princess—a daughter of the King of kings and Lord of lords.

> *I will be your Father, and you will be my sons and daughters, says the Lord Almighty.*
>
> —2 Corinthians 6:18 NLT

Beauty has its benefits, and being a Christian is the most beautiful benefit of all. You are loved, accepted, and treasured by your heavenly Father. You're Daddy's special girl, and don't you ever forget it!

> *God alone made it possible for you to be in Christ Jesus. For our benefit God made Christ to be wisdom itself. He is the one who made us acceptable to God. He made us pure and holy, and he gave himself to purchase our freedom.*
>
> —1 Corinthians 1:30 NLT

Prayer and Praise / Thankful Thoughts: _____

_____

_____

_____

Cleansing, toning, moisturizing, and occasional exfoliation are the necessary elements of proper skin care. However, you can practice other beauty behaviors that will benefit your skin as well. The following list of beauty bonuses can be adapted to almost any budget.

- When you cleanse, tone, moisturize, or exfoliate your face, use an upward, circular motion with your fingertips. Gravity is constantly pulling your skin down, so reverse the process by moving it up.

- Try new products at night before you go to bed. That way, if you experience an adverse reaction, your skin will have several hours to get over it.

- Radiant skin requires a balanced diet, regular exercise, plenty of water, and sufficient sleep. There isn't a skin-care routine in the world that can benefit you more than a healthy lifestyle.

- Cleanse your face before you exercise. Sweat will then naturally rid your pores of impurities, which means you'll need to cleanse it again after the workout. Also, make sure you tone and moisturize the second time around.

- Pull your hair back off your face before you wash it. This allows you to deep-clean your skin as well as keep oils, dirt, and products that are in your hair off your face.

- Change your pillowcase often. Pillowcases collect dirt and oil from your hair, which can get on your face and cause breakouts.

- If your face, hands, or feet are puffy, cut back on your salt intake. Soda pop, in particular, is one of the leading culprits.

- When you moisturize your face, don't forget your neck. Your neck will give your age away just as quickly as your face if it is not properly cared for.

- Exfoliate your lips by dabbing on some olive oil followed by a sprinkle of sugar. Gently rub your lips with your fingertip to remove chapped skin. Rinse and apply lip balm to smooth and protect.

- Moisturize your lips before you go to bed. Lips tend to dry out while you sleep, especially if you sleep with your mouth open.

- Mix your cleanser with warm water to open pores and remove dirt. Finish with a cool-water rinse to close your pores and block the dirt from getting in.

- If you still have mascara residue under your eyes after you wash your face, use an eye moisturizer to clean it up. This will not only remove the makeup but can help eliminate fine lines in the process.

MakeOver Minute #95
DETAILING

God has a plan for you, but it's up to you to detail your goals in order to reach your potential. You need to put into place what you wish to accomplish, back it with prayer, and then proceed as led.

1. **Plan:** What do you want to accomplish? Write your goals down, set a deadline, and follow God's lead. While you may have to readjust or rewrite your plans as you go along, at least you've entered the race.

   We can make our plans, but the LORD determines our steps.
   —Proverbs 16:9 NLT

2. **Pray:** Ask God to help you know what to do and how to do it. Any good runner gets coaching, and God is the ultimate Coach.

   Many plans are in the human heart, but the advice of the LORD will endure.
   —Proverbs 19:21 GOD'S WORD

3. **Proceed:** Do you make it happen, or do you let it happen? This is the difference between those who achieve goals and those who don't even try. Even if it's just the to-do list on the refrigerator, take steps to check it off. When you finish, you'll have a sense of accomplishment.

No matter the size and shape of the goal, when it's outlined according to God's purpose and plan, your life will be well-defined and you'll win in the end.

The steps of the godly are directed by the LORD. He delights in every detail of their lives.
—Psalm 37:23 NLT

Prayer and Praise / Thankful Thoughts: _____

_____

_____

_____

Using eyeliner is similar to outlining a picture in a coloring book. While a colored picture looks nice, it's the outlining that really makes the picture pop. The same is true of your eyes—color them with shadow and they look good, but frame them with liner and they look great!

Eyeliners come in pencils, creams, powders, and liquids. Liquid eyeliner is by far the most difficult to apply and should be left to the experts. Pencils, creams, and powders, on the other hand, are much more user-friendly. Pencils work just like a regular pencil, and creams and powders are applied with an eyeliner brush. To get started, pick your product of choice, then determine the shape of your eyes. The following advice will help you stay in line from there.

- **Close-set eyes:** Working outward, line both your upper and lower lids from the center of your eye. Gently blend.

- **Wide-set eyes:** Starting at the inside corner of your eye, line both the upper and lower lids two-thirds of the way across. Next, gently blend to the outer corners.

- **Deep-set eyes:** Line just the outer three-quarters of your eye on both the top and bottom, then blend.

- **Small, narrow eyes:** Line both your upper and lower lids from the center of your eyelid out. Extend the line from the outer edge upward and outward, then blend.

- **Large, round eyes:** Start at the inner corner of your upper lid and work toward the outer edge, extending the line outward and upward. Line only the outer corner beneath your eye, blending it upward and outward also.

- **None of the above:** Start at the inner corner of your eye and work your way to the outer edge. When you reach the corner, take the line slightly up and out. Follow this process on the upper and lower base of your lashes.

No matter what eye shape you're working with, use a 5x magnifying mirror to avoid drawing skimpy, incomplete lines. If you do miss a spot, simply go back and fill it in. Then gently smudge to blend.

MakeOver Minute #96
BROW RAISING

Beautifully shaped and colored brows complement both your eyes and face. Unfortunately, for most of us they do not come naturally. Every day pesky hairs grow outside the brow line, and if you don't stay on top of them your brows can easily get out of shape.

Did you know that what is true for your eyebrows is also true for your mind? If you don't constantly stay on top of your thinking, you can end up out of shape spiritually. Here's what the Bible says about it:

Don't become so well-adjusted to your culture that you fit into it without even thinking. Instead, fix your attention on God. You'll be changed from the inside out. Readily recognize what he wants from you, and quickly respond to it. Unlike the culture around you, always dragging you down to its level of immaturity, God brings the best out of you, develops well-formed maturity in you.

—Romans 12:2

Allow the Holy Spirit to transform your thinking. Browse your thoughts. Is there anything that does not line up with the Word of God? If so, pluck it from your mind. Aligning your thinking with God's wisdom will have a refining and shaping effect on your life.

Prayer and Praise / Thankful Thoughts: _____

_____

_____

_____

Well-groomed brows are the crowning touch to your eyes. Beautifully shaped brows frame your eyes, flatter your face, and give you an instant face-lift with just a tweeze. The right shape and color of brows can be a remarkable beauty asset, while the wrong ones can ruin even the prettiest face.

I meet gals all the time who go to great lengths to put on the perfect face, but do nothing at all when it comes to their brows. Yet raising the perfect eyebrow is not as hard as it seems. With just a little practice, you'll be able to meticulously shape, style, sketch, and set your brows just like the pros.

If you're going to care for your own brows, I recommend that you invest in a pair of Tweezerman flat-slant tweezers. This particular type has a good grip that is easy to control. You'll also need a good magnifying mirror. I use one that has 10x magnification, leaving no room for error.

1. **Shape:** The best time to tweeze your eyebrows is just after you have showered. Hot water opens your pores, allowing the hair to be removed more easily. Pull your skin taut, then use your tweezers to pull out one hair at a time. Go slowly, plucking out each stray hair. Single hair removal allows you to carefully study your progress as you go along so you don't overdo it.

2. **Style:** After you tweeze, use an eyebrow brush or child's toothbrush and sweep your brows upward so you can see if any need to be trimmed. Trim your brows with a pair of manicure scissors, cutting only one hair at a time and being careful not to cut them too short. This will allow the natural shape of your brow to develop.

3. **Sketch:** To apply eyebrow pencil—or powder, if you prefer—start at the inside and use feathery strokes, working your way out. Follow your natural brow line, carefully defining the arch as you go. If you have trouble filling in the bare spots, brush your brows inward and fill in with a pencil, then brush them back into place.

4. **Set:** Comb your brows into place, then set them with a dab of hair gel or clear mascara. Just put a small amount on the eyebrow brush and brush them into place.

MakeOver Minute #97
EYE CATCHING

Eye shadow is an outward expression, depicting a mood or style. However, the eyes' truest form of expression come from how you feel on the inside. The eyes are the mirrors of the soul. They communicate your thoughts and convey the intentions of your heart.

> *Your eye is a light for the body. When your eyes are good, your whole body will be full of light. But when your eyes are evil, your whole body will be full of darkness. So be careful not to let the light in you become darkness.*
>
> —Luke 11:34-35 NCV

Jesus brings life and light into this dark world. When you invite Him— the one true light—into your life, you become a reflection of the Light living in you. Jesus says in Matthew 5:14, "You are the light of the world. A city that is set on a hill cannot be hidden." He uses this word picture to illustrate how Christians are like neon signs living in a dark, sinful world in need of direction.

Your life is a light, and how you live it speaks volumes to those you come in contact with. Don't allow your light to dim, but instead fix your eyes on God and He will light the way for the world through you. So let your light shine!

Prayer and Praise / Thankful Thoughts: _____

_____

_____

_____

You don't have to spend a lot to make your eyes look beautiful. Eye shadow is an inexpensive way to have fun and be artistic with color. Eye shadows come in many colors and several different forms—powder, pencil, and cream. Personally, I like powder the best because it goes on smooth and is the easiest to blend.

Applying eye shadow can be intimidating until you get the hang of it, but with a little professional guidance, you can create a number of looks using only three colors. To get started, choose three matte colors of eye shadow that complement your skin tone and blend well with each other. For example, warm tones consist of earthy shades of olive green, gold, terra cotta, brown, coral, and ivory. Cool tones are made up of neutral tints of gray, taupe, mauve, plum, peach, and white.

As you choose your color palette, look for a light shade, a medium shade, and a darker shade. A sheer, light tint is good for the backdrop of the eyes. It acts as a foundation for your shadow, as this color will sweep from the base of your lashes to the bottom of your brow. The medium hue is great for your lid, and the darkest of the shades creates drama when applied to the crease of your eye. This is only one method. Below are other looks you can try using the same three colors and one eye-shadow brush.

- **All-natural gal:** Apply the lightest shadow from the base of your lash line to your brow, then apply the medium shade in the crease of your lid. Gently blend.

- **Drama queen:** Apply the lightest hue from your lash line to the bottom of your brow, then apply the medium shade over your lid. Next, add the darkest shade to the crease and blend upward toward the outer corners of your eye up to the brow bone.

- **Classy lady:** Apply the lightest shadow from your lashes to your brow, then apply the medium shadow to the inside corners of your eyelids, sweeping and blending outward.

- **Flirty chick:** For those special times with your husband, apply the lightest color from your lash line to the base of your brow, then apply the medium shade to the outer corners of your eyelids, blending upward toward your brow bone. Sweep on a hint of the darkest shade to the outer brow bone and blend.

MakeOver Minute #98
EYE PLEASING

When applied correctly, eye shadow can balance the eyes by reshaping and redefining with just the stroke of a shadow. The eye shadow filters what we see so our perceived faults become visually flawless.

Shadowing our eyes is important in other ways. We must be careful with what we look at in order to remain faultless and flawless before the Lord. Remember this little song?

> O be careful little eyes what you see,
> O be careful little eyes what you see,
> For the Father up above is looking down with love.
> So, be careful little eyes what you see.

Experts say that an image is seared into your mind for 20-plus years, and the more often you recall the image, the more permanent it becomes. The Bible says, "If therefore your eye is good, your body will be full of light. But if your eye is bad, your body will be full of darkness" (Luke 11:34-35). What are you looking at? Are you filling the files of your mind with lightness or darkness?

God's Word directs us on where to set our sights:

> *Summing it all up, friends, I'd say you'll do best by filling your minds and meditating on things true, noble, reputable, authentic, compelling, gracious—the best, not the worst; the beautiful, not the ugly; things to praise, not things to curse.*
>
> —Philippians 4:8

Redefine and reshape your life by shadowing your eyes from sin and focusing them on the things of God. When your eyes please Him, your body will be full of light, and you will be the light that gives light to the world.

Prayer and Praise / Thankful Thoughts: _____

_____

_____

_____

In our previous MakeOver Minute, we talked about how to use eye shadows to express mood and style. Here, we're going to learn about shape and dimension and discover how to successfully create illusions using the same three eye shadows. With just a stroke of a brush, you can easily overshadow any faults you perceive your eyes to have.

Two basic techniques are used to enhance the natural size and shape of one's eyes—highlighting and shading. Highlighting emphasizes, while shading visually diminishes. Teamed together, they can work wonders. To get a better idea of how to make your eyes look a certain way, follow these eye-pleasing tips.

- **Close-set eyes:** Apply a neutral, medium color from your lash line to your brow, then apply the darker shade to the outer corner of your eyelids. Next, highlight the outer half of your brow bone with the lightest shadow and blend.

- **Wide-set eyes:** Apply a neutral, medium shadow from the base of your lashes to the bottom of your brow, then apply the darkest shadow in the crease from the middle of your lid inward. Next, gently blend from the inside corner of your eye upward toward your brow. Using the lightest hue, highlight the outer two-thirds of the brow arch.

- **Deep-set eyes:** Apply a neutral, medium shadow from your lash line to the base of your brow, then apply the darker shadow just above the crease of your lid and blend upward. Apply the lightest shadow on your lid, then finish by using the same shadow to highlight just beneath your brow.

- **Small, narrow eyes:** Apply a neutral, light shadow from the lashes to your brow. Then apply the medium shadow to your eyelid and the darkest shadow from the middle of your crease outward and blend.

- **Large, round eyes:** Apply a neutral, medium shadow from your lash line to the base of your brow. Apply the darkest shadow to the crease of your eye, blending outward to the corner of your eye and up. Highlight the base of your brow bone with the lightest tint.

MakeOver Minute #99
POWDER PUFF

Powder gives your face a fresh, flawless finish. Its lucidity prevents makeup meltdown with a transparent shield of protection. Whether worn over foundation or alone, it leaves a sheer, see-through finish and improves the natural radiance of your skin.

Transparency is the defining issue. It's what lets the real you shine through. No more pretending. It's all about being honest with yourself and truthful with others.

Being a phony never works. It has an effect just the opposite of what you'd hoped for. Instead of building up, it knocks you down. At first people may be impressed, but after a while they'll just get turned off. Being real is what works.

Clothe yourselves with humility toward one another, for God is opposed to the proud, but gives grace to the humble.

—1 Peter 5:5 NASB

If you puff yourself up, you'll get the wind knocked out of you. But if you're content to simply be yourself, your life will count for plenty.

—Matthew 23:12

Prayer and Praise / Thankful Thoughts: _____

_____

_____

_____

Powder is the one cosmetic you won't want to be caught without. It can be worn on bare skin to combat oily shine or dusted lightly over foundation and concealer to give your skin a smooth surface in preparation for a little blusher. If you happen to put on too much blusher, blending in a little powder will remedy that too!

Powders come in two forms—loose or pressed. Loose powder is sold in a jarlike container and is applied with a large powder brush. Pressed powder comes in a solid form, pressed into a compact, and is applied with a powder puff. Both are a great investment. Loose powder is great for when you first apply your makeup, and pressed powder is a must for on-the-go touch-ups throughout the course of your day.

Powders offer various degrees of coverage. Some are formulated to give a sheer, translucent finish, while others are designed to buff into the skin and even out its tone. The one you choose depends on whether you're using it as a base or using it to set your foundation. Powders also come in a wide range of colors. In fact, many companies manufacture powders to perfectly match the shades of their foundation. Here are formulas from which to choose.

- **Matte finish:** Matte powders have a dense consistency that neutralizes skin discolorations and reduces oily shine. They can be worn alone or over foundation. Due to their heavy texture, they should be dusted on lightly in order to avoid caking.

- **Sheer finish:** Powders with a sheer finish highlight the skin with a light, reflective glaze of see-through color. They set foundation and concealer and blend easily for lightweight coverage.

- **Translucent finish:** Translucent powders create a no-glow effect that perfectly sets makeup. It's best to lightly dust it across your face after you've applied makeup but before you apply mascara so you don't dull your lashes.

- **Shimmery or iridescent finish:** Shimmery or iridescent powder is a subtle way of adding a pearl-like sparkle to your cheekbones, décolletage, and shoulders. Do not use it on your entire face.

- **Light-diffusing finish:** A light-diffusing finish is designed to minimize the appearance of imperfections so your skin looks less lined and more radiant. Special ingredients diffuse light as it hits your skin, creating a luminous finish.

MakeOver Minute #100
READ MY LIPS

Beautiful lips express a mood, accentuate your makeup, and accessorize your wardrobe. But they can quickly turn ugly depending on what you say and how you say it. Lips can be either your most glamorous asset or your most unattractive drawback.

The words you speak and the tone you use can provoke a vast vocabulary of emotions—love, encouragement, hostility, criticism, help, healing, tension, or frustration. What you say sticks, and once you give your words away, you can't take them back.

> *Set a guard, O LORD, over my mouth; keep*
> *watch over the door of my lips.*
>
> —Psalm 141:3 NKJV

The answer to saying the right thing at the precise time with the ideal tone can be found in the perfect **LIPS.**

- **L**isten to what you're going to say before you say it. Think before you speak.

- **I**mprove your vocabulary. Increase your intellect by increasing your vocabulary.

- **P**ray for discernment. Ask God to help you say the right thing, in the right way.

- **S**peak two positives for every negative thing you say. Be an encourager, not a discourager.

Apply to your lips *kindness,* and you'll be kind. Apply to them *encouragement,* and you'll be an encourager. Apply to them *compliments,* and you'll be admired for your lovely lips!

Prayer and Praise / Thankful Thoughts: _____

_____

_____

_____

Beautiful lips speak volumes. Lips highlight our smiles, frame our words, express our affection, and even accent our wardrobe when we accessorize them with color. Lipstick is the one cosmetic you can experiment with over and over again, repeatedly changing your look simply by trying new colors—you're only limited by your own creativity.

Lipsticks and liners come in a seemingly endless array of colors and formulas. Finding what you want—or need—can be more involved than ever, but with a few hints, you'll know just what to look for.

1. **Choose a color** based on your skin tone—either warm or cool. Warm complexions look best in shades of coral, ginger, orange-red, and brown. Cool skin tones look most excellent in pink, raisin, blue-red, and berry. As you choose your color, consider the clothing you're wearing. The colors should complement, not clash with, each another.

2. **Choose the type and texture** of your lip color based on the look you want to achieve.

   - *Matte* finishes give full, intense coverage and offer the best wear. They can, however, stain your lips.

   - *Glossy* finishes look sheer and shiny and wear off easily. They can be worn alone or over other lip color.

   - *Satin* finishes give medium to full coverage with just a touch of shine.

   - *Frost* finishes give light to medium coverage with lots of shimmer. On the downside, this type of formula highlights flaws.

   - *Sheer* finishes give lips translucent color with just a bit of shine.

   - *Long-lasting* finishes are designed to stay on until you take them off. However, the results vary, and the formulas can be quite drying.

   - *Volumizing* finishes plump up your lips with micro-injected collagen, while diminishing fine lines and wrinkles around the lip line.

To apply lip color, follow these basic steps:

1. With a lip liner, draw in the V—or bow—of your lip, then line the lip from the V to the outer corners. For the lower lip, begin in the center and work your way out to the corners.

2. Next, apply your lipstick. Use a lip brush to blend so there is no visible liner line.

3. Finish with a little gloss or shimmer. You're ready to go!

MakeOver Minute #101
KEEPING UP APPEARANCES

We spend countless hours keeping up our appearance—perfect hair, well-chosen makeup, trendy accessories, a flattering wardrobe. We learn all the tricks of the trade to enhance, reduce, refine, and highlight our best features as we downplay, conceal, mask, and hide the features we're not so fond of. We scour the malls, peruse magazines, and quiz the experts for beauty advice, but what we really need is to get into the Word of God.

I want women to show their beauty by dressing in appropriate clothes that are modest and respectable. Their beauty will be shown by what they do, not by their hair styles or the gold jewelry, pearls, or expensive clothes they wear. This is what is proper for women who claim to have reverence for God.

—1 Timothy 2:9-10 GOD'S WORD

Lately, I've been a guest on a number of call-in radio programs throughout the United States and Canada. Without fail, I always receive phone calls from frustrated men who are concerned about women of all ages dressing immodestly for church. These men relate how difficult it is for them. They express feelings of guilt, and they're disturbed about how this issue hinders their worship. One guy put it this way: "How am I supposed to focus on God when the girl in front of me is hanging out all over the place and making me feel like a dirty old man?"

Ladies, there is a fine line between looking good in a respectable fashion and looking good in a sexy sort of way. All of us like to look and feel our best, but we should never do this at the expense of others. We need to consider if what we are wearing is provocative in any manner whatsoever. We do not want our obsession with fashion to become an obstacle to the opposite sex.

It's not a sin to want to look attractive, but what really matters is how you appear to God. True beauty begins on the inside, and there is no way to fake it with your Lord. He knows your heart. Clothe yourself with reverence to God, respect for yourself, and consideration for others, and you'll always project a beautiful appearance from the inside out.

*What matters is not your outer appearance—
the styling of your hair, the jewelry you wear, the cut of
your clothes—but your inner disposition.*
—1 Peter 3:3-4

Prayer and Praise / Thankful Thoughts: _____

_____

_____

_____

Keeping up appearances can be a challenge when you're faced with body issues that skew your style. All of us have figure concerns that need special attention, and you can dress to disguise with just a little creativity. Use the following fashion fixes to "mock up" just the right look.

- To **look thinner,** wear the same color on top and bottom. This creates a vertical line, which makes you look slimmer. Draw the eye upward toward your face with great-looking jewelry, and avoid full skirts, pleats, and any bulk where you don't want it or need it.

- **Create length** by dressing in a monochromatic color scheme. Dressing in the same color from head to toe prevents horizontal breaks that cut you in half and make you look shorter.

- To **make yourself appear shorter,** create visual breakdown by wearing one color on top and another on the bottom. Accessorize with a wide belt, and use large prints and patterns to scale down height, while avoiding dressing in all one color.

- **Lengthen a short waist** by wearing the same color on top and bottom to bring continuity to your look. Try drop-waist tops or dresses and longer-styled jackets. Stay away from wide belts and short tops and jackets.

- **Shorten a long waist** by wearing empire-style tops, wide belts, and short jackets. Avoid drop waists and hip-cut belts.

- **Enhance your bustline** and create fullness up top by wearing a push-up bra and layering your clothing. Or wear a brightly colored shirt and dark-colored pants to slim your bottom and enlarge your top, giving the illusion of fullness. Stay away from clingy, low-cut tops.

- **Minimize a full bust** by wearing a V-neck top. The V-shape visually opens up to your face, drawing attention away from your bustline. Accent your face with great earrings and jewelry, and stay away from ruffles, horizontal stripes, and any top with beads, bows, or bling across the bustline.

- **Make your neck look longer or shorter** with a few simple tricks. To visually lengthen your neck, accent it with an open collar or V-neck, and steer clear of scarves, necklaces, and turtlenecks—anything that draws attention to the neck area. To shorten your neck, do just the opposite. Wear items that conceal the neck, such as turtlenecks, cowl necks, scarves, and necklaces.

- **Narrow broad shoulders** by eliminating shoulder pads and using scarves, necklaces, or V-neck tops to draw attention toward your center area. Widen narrow shoulders with shoulder pads and boat-neck tops.

- **Slenderize thick arms** with loose-fitting sleeves. Stay away from sleeveless shirts, cropped sleeves, and clingy fabrics.

- **Slim down your bottom** with a showy shirt or fabulous jewelry that draws attention up top. Wear dark, neutral colors on the bottom half and avoid pleats, plaids, patterns, and stripes.

- **Elongate your legs** by wearing all one color on your bottom half, including hosiery and shoes. Avoid cropped or capri pants, which make your legs look shorter.

- **Shorten long legs** with the use of patterned bottoms, cropped or capri pants, and longer tops that fall just below the hips. Avoid high-waisted pants and skirts, which only add to the length.

~ ~ ~

Just One Minute More

Being beautiful is not just about hairdos, pedicures, lip color, and stylish clothes—true beauty is a matter of the heart. Internal glamour is a "soul" attribute that is evident in those who are composed and confident in who they are in relationship to Jesus Christ.

A makeover from the inside out has lasting effects. It is ageless, timeless, and everlasting. Outer beauty will fade with time, but remember, inner beauty flourishes forever.

Charm can mislead and beauty soon fades.
The woman to be admired and praised is the woman
who lives in the Fear-of-God.
—Proverbs 31:30

~ ~ ~

Other good books about lifestyles and attitudes that work together

Want to gain energy, lose weight, and enjoy better health?

With this positive, can-do approach, you can gain maximum health while losing excess pounds. You'll discover...

- why runaway blood sugar is a key factor in food cravings and weight issues

- how blood-sugar problems lead to damage to your body

- ways to evaluate pre-diabetes health risks, such as hypoglycemia

- reasons and motivation to change your life-style

- diet and exercise that really work

Whether you are diabetic, have a family history of diabetes, or are simply tired of being sick and tired, *Overcoming Runaway Blood Sugar* may very well change the way you view eating and exercise forever.

Renew your mind,
rejuvenate your body

Would you like to increase your flexibility, improve your circulation, and enhance your level of energy? Finally there's a program that offers proven stretching and flexibility exercises without troubling Eastern influences. Now you can fill your mind with the Word of God as you practice the postures on this DVD that will

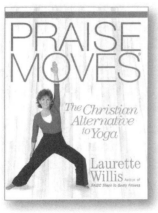

- promote healing and overall physical health

- relieve stress and enhance relaxation

- glorify God with your spirit, soul, and body

Certified personal trainer Laurette Willis shows you a way to transform your workouts into worship with *PraiseMoves*®!

"All he wants is sex, sex, sex!"

If it seems like you and your husband are operating on different wavelengths, there's a good reason for it. God designed the differences between you and your husband to draw you together, points out Marla Taviano. So there's a lot you can do to make sex work *for* your relationship. With that positive in mind, Marla helps you to...

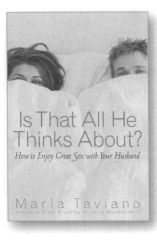

- stop the "meet my needs; then I'll meet yours" mind-set

- expect your husband to act like a man, not like a woman

- celebrate God's plan for you, as a woman, to be godly and sexual

- find forgiveness for a wrong sexual past

- discover fun, creative ideas for more frequent "wows" in the bedroom...and a future filled with the pleasure, joy, and closeness you've always hoped for

∽ ∽ ∽

To read sample chapters from these and other Harvest House books, go to www.harvesthousepublishers.com